Flexible Implementation:
A Key to Asia's Transformation

Policy Studies
an East-West Center series

Series Editors
Dieter Ernst and Marcus Mietzner

Description
Policy Studies presents scholarly analysis of key contemporary domestic
and international political, economic, and strategic issues affecting Asia
in a policy relevant manner. Written for the policy community, academics, journalists, and the informed public, the peer-reviewed publications in this series provide new policy insights and perspectives based
on extensive fieldwork and rigorous scholarship.

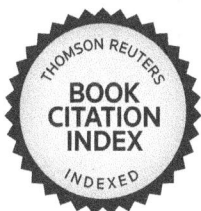

The East-West Center is pleased to announce that
the Policy Studies series has been accepted for in-
dexing in Web of Science Book Citation Index.
The Web of Science is the largest and most com-
prehensive citation index available.

Notes to Contributors
Submissions may take the form of a proposal or complete manuscript.
For more information on the Policy Studies series, please contact the
Series Editors.

Editors, Policy Studies
East-West Center
1601 East-West Road
Honolulu, Hawai'i 96848-1601
Tel: 808.944.7197
Publications@EastWestCenter.org
EastWestCenter.org/PolicyStudies

Policy
Studies | 70

Flexible Implementation:
A Key to Asia's Transformation

Luke Simon Jordan and Katerina Koinis

Flexible Implementation: A Key to Asia's Transformation
Luke Simon Jordan and Katerina Koinis

ISSN 1547-1349 (print) and 1547-1330 (electronic)
ISBN 978-0-86638-248-9 (print) and 978-0-86638-249-6 (electronic)

The content of this volume is a product of the staff of the International Bank for Reconstruction and Development/The World Bank. The findings, interpretations, and conclusions expressed in this paper do not necessarily reflect the views of the Executive Directors of The World Bank or the governments they represent. The World Bank does not guarantee the accuracy of the data included in this work. The boundaries, colors, denominations, and other information shown on any map in this work do not imply any judgment on the part of The World Bank concerning the legal status of any territory or the endorsement or acceptance of such boundaries.

The views expressed are those of the author(s) and not necessarily those of the East-West Center.

Hard copies of all titles, and free electronic copies of most titles, are available from:

Publication Sales Office
East-West Center
1601 East-West Road
Honolulu, Hawai'i 96848-1601
Tel: 808.944.7145
Fax: 808.944.7376
EWCBooks@EastWestCenter.org
EastWestCenter.org/PolicyStudies

In Asia, hard copies of all titles, and electronic copies of select Southeast Asia titles, co-published in Singapore, are available from:

Institute of Southeast Asian Studies
30 Heng Mui Keng Terrace
Pasir Panjang Road, Singapore 119614
publish@iseas.edu.sg
bookshop.iseas.edu.sg

Contents

List of Acronyms

ARPA-E   Advanced Research Projects Agency-Energy, US Department of Energy

BAA   broad agency announcement

CGP   Commissariat General du Plan, France

DARPA   Defense Advanced Research Projects Agency, US Department of Defense

DoD   Department of Defense, United States

EPB   Economic Planning Board, Korea

GP   general partner

GPS   global positioning system

IARPA   Intelligence Advanced Research Projects Activity, US Director of National Intelligence

IbIn   India Backbone Implementation Network

IBM   International Business Machines Corporation

IPO   Initial Public Offering

IT   information technology

LBO   leveraged buy-out

LP	limited partner
MIT	Massachusetts Institute of Technology
MITI	Ministry of International Trade and Industry, Japan
NEDA	National Economic Development Agency, the Philippines
NSF	National Science Foundation
OD	office director (DARPA)
PARC	Palo Alto Research Center (Xerox)
PM	program manager (DARPA)
PMDU	Prime Minister's Delivery Unit, United Kingdom
POSCO	(formerly) Pohang Iron and Steel Company
R&D	research and development
RFP	request for proposal
UK	United Kingdom
US	United States
VC	venture capital

Executive Summary

Despite the region's economic growth over the last few decades, countries across Asia still face the complex challenge of structural transformation. Low-income economies must build formal industrial and service sectors from agricultural and informal bases; middle-income economies must move up the value chain; and high-income economies must continually generate new capabilities at the frontier of innovation.

Meeting this challenge requires implementing and adjusting solutions addressing a range of problems—problems whose complexities imply often it cannot be known *ex ante* whether proposed solutions will succeed or fail. Agencies tasked with delivering rapid growth—or similarly difficult tasks—must be able to act both effectively and nimbly: trying potential solutions, discarding sub-optimal ones, and reallocating resources quickly.

The prerequisite for such "learning by doing" is flexibility. This is a capacity easy to advocate but hard to build.

Flexibility is a capacity easy to advocate but hard to build

This study therefore focuses on *how* real-world policymakers might operationalize the capability to be flexible in the agencies they lead or create. Since such agencies may alternatively be *ineffectively* flexible, withdrawing support too soon or incurring inordinate political costs in doing so, this study begins by identifying four issues which must be tackled to maintain flexibility *and* effectiveness:

- *Uncertainty*—How to know which initiatives to back and how to differentiate between likely failures and future success with temporary troubles.
- *Exit costs*—How to manage the non-financial risks and costs of acknowledging failure, in particular the political costs.
- *Governing discretion*—How to provide agencies with discretionary use of resources without opening them to shirking or capture.
- *Using discretion*—How agencies should use such day-to-day discretion once it is granted.

The study examines in detail a range of organizations facing these issues to different degrees. It first considers firms managing venture capital funds, particularly their methods of decision-making. Second, this study considers the Defense Advanced Research Projects Agency (DARPA) within the US Department of Defense. Third, this study considers the Ministry of International Trade and Industry (MITI) of Japan, along with a brief review of other "navigating agencies" steering industrial policy.

Drawing on primary interviews and existing literature, it asks of each the following questions: What techniques—formal and informal—do relatively successful flexible agencies use? What kinds of overall environments—and what manner of links to them—make these techniques more or less effective?

Based on the answers to these questions, this study identifies a set of fourteen structural characteristics and techniques contributing to flexible implementation.

Among the most prominent are the importance of fixed, measurable, and unambiguous long-term goals; the conscious use of surrounding networks of other institutions and partners; exceptional focus on managing and using thick flows of information; and a common sequence of responses to potential failure. Some of the identified techniques—including the use of quantitative targets as instruments of problem solving rather than of rigid accountability—diverge from certain folk wisdoms of public management.

This study concludes by tentatively aggregating this pattern of features and techniques into three potential strategies for flexibility. These are:

1. *Tiered and differentiated decision-making*—Agencies should be given clear and unambiguous goals which matter to the survival of the political elite. Agencies should then differentiate between "programs" (new and visionary concepts to achieve goals) and "approaches" (specific actions attempting to implement these concepts). The approval process for the first should protect against errors of commission while the approval process for the second should protect against errors of omission. This might also be characterized as *gradated and disciplined autonomy.*

2. *Acting through a (shaped) system*—Agencies are created within surrounding systems whose resources—human, intellectual, and financial—must be leveraged. The nodes of these surrounding systems must be extended, combined, and induced by these agencies to create both the *capabilities* and *coalitions* needed for success—with these actions incentivized by the promise of access to incremental resources.

3. *Information overload*—Agencies and their superiors must emphasize information transmittal through formal and informal meetings and processes. Accountability must be less for the failure of an approach than for not knowing or understanding the causes for the failure or for not being able to extract useful information from any failures.

In sum: disciplined autonomy, indirect action, and information-centric management. Of critical importance is recognizing that these strategies are interdependent. One cannot manage complex systems without information and autonomy. Political costs would likely be insurmountable for granting autonomy to agencies supplied with adequate resources and authority to act directly at sufficient scale—no matter the level of "political will" available.

Indeed, the obsession with "political will" in some parts of current policy discourse seems, in light of these strategies, misplaced. Equally so does the vogue for "private sector" solutions. Neither DARPA nor MITI had direct reporting lines to the heads of their respective governments—and venture capital firms resemble these public institutions far more than they resemble leveraged buy-out firms—their private cousins.

Practical implications of these strategies suggest three core tasks for political leaders and policymakers seeking to create or reform navigating agencies to address Asia's uncertain policy challenges, including:

1. Defining clear, unambiguous, and easy-to-measure long-range goals whose failure would threaten the survival of political elites—and linking tiered-approval processes to these goals.
2. Defining the systems in which these agencies will be embedded and obtaining for these agencies the financial and/or political resources allowing them both autonomy and the ability to shape and to induce actions within their surrounding systems.
3. Establishing management processes that generate thick information flows and making managing these thick information flows the day-to-day accountability of these agencies.

The difficulty of each of these tasks, the first in particular, should not be underestimated. Each requires expertise in institution building, people management, and rhetoric and politics. Given the complexity of problems confronting leaders and policymakers over the next decade, in Asia and elsewhere, and the extraordinary results achieved by flexible and effective agencies, however, one might argue that few tasks could be more important.

Flexible Implementation:
A Key to Asia's Transformation

Introduction

Motivation

Despite the rapid economic growth of the last few decades, countries across Asia still face the complex task of achieving structural transformation. Achieving this will require a wide range of policy issues to be addressed—over time and across multiple sectors.

Human capital must be built; infrastructure designed and constructed; access to finance enabled; and technology transferred. A broad base of firms must come into existence; self-discover the true costs of production; acquire capabilities; and move toward the global quality frontier. Policy instruments supporting firms in doing so must also discipline them so that the most productive firms expand, thus helping both incomes and jobs to rise together. This challenge is daunting. It is also dynamic. Solving one set of problems creates outcomes which, in turn, produce additional problems. Achieving individual successes through focus must be scaled up before they can make a substantive difference to overall growth.[1]

Making national economic growth happen is thus a formidable managerial challenge. The diversity, scale, and difficulty of tasks are well beyond anything faced by almost any private-sector firm or other organization. The problems are so technically complex it is almost impossible to know with certainty whether the outcome will be successful. As Ben Bernanke (2013) recently put it: "[In politics,] honest error in the face of complex and possibly intractable problems is a far more important source of bad results than are bad motives ...[and] economics is a highly sophisticated field of thought that is superb at explaining to policymakers precisely why the choices they made in the past were wrong. About the future, not so much."

This pervasive uncertainty about what will work and what will not work requires implementation, particularly in industrial policy, to be a process of experimentation and learning (Rodrik 2008). The problem, then, is who—if anyone—manages this process, and how.

Typologies

For most rapidly industrialized economies, the answer to the "who" question posed above is clear: Their histories reveal that dedicated bodies managed such sets of programs (and investments). These have been called various names: "nodal agencies," "reform teams," "delivery units," or "backbone organizations"—with institutional forms ranging from ministries to autonomous agencies to informal teams (Criscuolo and Palmade 2008; Watkins et al. 2010). They share a mandate—explicit or implicit—to bring about structural change. Beyond this shared mandate they vary in multiple dimensions, from formalization to reporting lines (Table 1).

They vary in their endowment of capital: political (primarily in the sense of access and authority) and financial (their own budget or authority over the budgets of others). Some have a high degree of political capital but a low level of financial resources (e.g., "delivery teams") while others confront the reverse situation (e.g., for much of its history, the Ministry of International Trade and Industry [MITI] in Japan), while a limited number have had both (e.g., the Economic Planning Board [EPB] in Korea).

These dedicated bodies also vary in the degree of uncertainty or risk attached to the solutions they pursue. All of them faced uncertainty—but some focused more on questions of discipline, delivering policies whose benefits and design were relatively clear, while others focused more on problems whose solution was not known, attempting multiple policies and flexibly adjusting between them.[2]

Table 1. Types of Agencies Pursuing Structural Transformation

Degree of structure	Moderate	High	Low	Low	Low	High
Reporting line	Head of State or Government	Head of Government	Head of Government	Public-Private Trust	Head of Government	Head of Government
Independence	Low	High	High	High	Low	Moderate
Financial capital	Low	High	Low	Low	Low	High
Political capital	High	Moderate	Moderate	Low	High	Moderate
Flexibility/discipline	Flexibility	Flexibility	Flexibility	Flexibility	Discipline	Discipline
Example	*Blue House Secretariat, Korea*	*MITI, Japan*	*CGP, France*	*IbIn, India*	*PMDU, UK*	*EPB, Korea[3]*

These variations in focus shape the capabilities such agencies must possess. Agencies may commit two types of errors: a) rejecting programs which could have been solutions or b) selecting and/or continuing investment in programs destined to fail.

Following Sah and Stiglitz (1986), this study identifies these errors as "type I" or "type II," respectively. In theory, agencies searching for solutions will care more about avoiding type I errors than agencies which believe they know the solutions and must conserve political resources to implement these known solutions. Such preferences should then influence how decisions are made.

More generally, confidence that solutions are known will lead to a focus on "delivery" with an emphasis (in the classic Weberian formulation) on rules, hierarchy, and discipline. The absence of such confidence will put a greater premium on "flexibility": the ability to try many things and to reorient action rapidly in response to new information.

This study then focuses on *how* real-world policymakers might operationalize the capability to be flexible. It is motivated by the argument above that the problems of industrial policy are particularly prone to requiring flexibility instead of discipline and by historical records of successes and failures, especially those in Asia. To take two canonical examples: Meiji-era Japan had a clear vision of what industries it sought to develop and addressed continual errors in "how" by flexibly adjusting policies to correct for mistakes (Jansen 2009; Crawcour 1989; Yamamura 1967), while Korea (under Park Chung-Hee) undertook wrenching changes in policy direction, sometimes as quickly as within two years, as it sought to emulate Japan with very different means (Kim and Vogel 2011).

Flexibility is a capability extremely useful well beyond any narrowly conceived industrial policy. Flexibility can be equally achievable and equally valuable in policy areas such as advanced-technology research. It may also be deployed in the context of larger policy issues requiring adaptive coordination and changes in direction—such as those involving regional cooperation or such global issues as climate change. Given the number, range, and complexity of such issues across Asia and the developing world, there is an urgent need to go beyond a simple call for the public sector to be more "nimble," to understand how flexibility comes about in practice, and how to build organizations possessing it.

Methodology

This study is meant to offer an initial step towards understanding organizational flexibility. It considers an agency to be more flexible the more often the agency reallocates resources among potential solutions to a given problem, focusing on the bodies shown on the left side of Table 1, which it will term "navigating agencies." Such agencies may also be *ineffectively* flexible, withdrawing support too soon or incurring such political costs as to lose their autonomy. In maintaining flexibility *and* effectiveness, four related issues must be tackled:[4]

- *Uncertainty*—How to know which initiatives or firms to back, and, post-selection, how to differentiate between likely failures and future success with temporary troubles;
- *Exit costs*—How to manage the non-financial risks and costs of acknowledging failure;
- *Governing discretion*—How to provide agencies with discretionary use of resources without opening them to shirking or capture; and
- *Using discretion*—What agencies should do with discretion once they have it. In particular, identifying how to improve the chances a program or investment will become a success once it is launched and how to respond to potential failure in ways other than exiting the initiative.

When framed in this manner it is possible to identify other organizations, beyond those mandating structural growth and beyond the public sector, having faced these same issues.

Some have pursued path-breaking research, with all its risks and uncertainties. Perhaps the canonical example of that approach is the Defense Advanced Research Projects Agency (DARPA) within the US Department of Defense.

Other organizations have sought exceptional investment returns. Outstanding examples of that approach are venture capital (VC) firms.

Across such organizations, of course, the intensity of these issues can be expected to vary. Venture capital firms, for example, face much lower exit costs than do public sector agencies—but they similarly face issues of uncertainty and management. A tentative typology of these highly flexible organizations is presented in Table 2.

Table 2. Types of Agencies with a High Degree of Flexibility			
Mandate	Structural transformation	Research breakthroughs	Exceptional returns
Public/private	Public	Public	Private
Uncertainty	Moderate	Exceptional	High
Exit Costs	Exceptional	Moderate	Low
Management	High	High	High
Example	*Navigating agencies*	*DARPA*	*Venture capital firms*

This study will first analyze the techniques of venture capital firms and DARPA before returning to navigating agencies *per se.* Methodologically, it is an exercise in theory-building and aims to build not a theory of general laws but one of contexts and contributing causes to certain outcomes (George and Bennett 2005). It does not presume to offer a general thesis or define a set of "best practices"—instead it provides a thorough description and a tentative set of patterns which may "help to fertilize judgment and experience, improving the prospects of policy implementation" (Corbett 1911).

> *This study does not presume to offer a general thesis or define a set of 'best practices,' but to identify patterns that may help to fertilize judgment, thereby improving the prospects of implementation*

To attempt this goal, this study will pose these questions of each organization:

- What techniques—formal and informal—do relatively successful flexible agencies use?
- What kinds of overall environments—and what manner of links to them—make these techniques more effective?

The first question will be split into "formal techniques" and "informal techniques"; the second question will be labeled as that of "structural characteristics." Following this "Introduction," these questions will be examined in the realm of venture capital firms in "Venture Capital Firms: The *Ne Plus Ultra* of Flexibility," followed by the example of DARPA in "The Curious Case of DARPA." In "Navigating Agencies," these findings will become the basis for comparisons to various navigating agencies, both successes and failures, with particular attention given to MITI. "Conclusions" offers final thoughts and an overall analysis of the attributes, capabilities, and trends discerned in this research.

Venture Capital Firms: The *Ne Plus Ultra* of Flexibility

The role of the venture capital (VC) industry in catalyzing some forms of innovation and promoting growth is well-documented—even if some analysts (especially since the "dot-com" implosion of 2001) have questioned the industry's ability to generate market-beating financial returns (Tett 2013). Other analysts have pointed out that the venture capital industry in the United States is not a panacea for the broader problems in US competitiveness, especially those in manufacturing (Berger 2013). The industry has been extensively studied, particularly the policy measures that may stimulate it, as have the firms in which it invests (Hwang and Horowitt 2012; Robles 2011).

Less attention has been paid to the industry's central agents: those firms that manage capital and invest it in other firms. Data availability is partly to blame—these firms have few requirements for disclosure and databases tracking VC investments are not always reliable (Kaplan, Strömberg, and Sensoy 2002).[5]

It has been shown, however, that returns in the industry are heavily skewed by a small number of investments radically out-performing the wider market and that these returns are fundamentally dependent on equity markets prone to bubbles (Janeway 2012).

This study will neither attempt to argue for or against venture capital's importance nor to define general rules regarding better- or worse-performing firms. Rather it will try to discern some of the ways in which these firms operate—in the belief that doing so may offer insights regarding the allocation of resources across a portfolio under conditions of extreme uncertainty. This may seem counterintuitive: VC firms assume, after all, that some investments will fail. Recognizing failure is assumed to be prohibitively costly, if not fatal, in the public sector. In other words, VC firms might be assumed to have solved, *a priori,* the core problem in flexibility.

However, though exit costs for a VC firm are low, they are not non-existent.[6] In addition, VC firms still face the issues of uncertainty and discretion almost as acutely as do navigating agencies. This is vividly drawn out by comparisons of VC to ordinary credit lending or even to "leveraged buy-outs" (LBOs)—the latter being a close cousin of VC within the universe of "private equity" investing.

As industry insiders describe them, LBO funds are built around rigid processes and targets while VC firms are built around flexibility (Hwang 2012). Being in the private sector, even in high-risk finance, is not a license to fail. Even compared to firms they resemble closely, VC firms are unusually flexible.

Description

The industry's formal unit is the venture capital fund. Funds are provided with most of their financial capital by "limited partners" (LPs). Funds are managed by venture capital firms. Venture capital firms consist of a small number of "general partners" (GPs) and their staff.[7] LPs do not give capital to VC firms: they give capital to VC funds which are managed by VC firms. These firms, however, have wide discretion during the fund's lock-up period, often ten years, during which LPs may not withdraw their capital (Waldeck, Wainwright, and Blaydon 2003). If a fund's performance is promising, at the five-year mark the GPs often begin to raise a new fund. The highest-performing firms will raise new funds even more rapidly: New Enterprise Associates, for example, has raised fourteen funds in thirty-five years.

VC firms invest in the equity of other companies, here called "investees." As they grow, investees typically raise funds in tranches. These are often designated as "Series A," "Series B," and so on. Different VC firms may specialize in earlier or later stages in this sequence. A single fund rarely holds more than 20 percent of an investee's equity. Most VC firms are said to target a distribution of returns of around one-fifth to two-fifths of investments failing; a similar number with low-to-neutral returns; "solid" returns for most of the remaining; and one or two "home runs" earning large multiples of the initial invest-ment.[8]

Within this system it might seem that hierarchy and market dis-cipline, reflected in returns, would simplify relationships and orient them toward technical concerns alone.

However, with a small number of GPs exercising wide discretion, "small group dynamics" take on substantial importance. Each GP has a stake of personal prestige before his or her peers in the success of "'their" investment as well as usually having a great deal more infor-mation about that specific investment than his or her peers. Each GP could thus seek to allocate disproportionate resources to an underper-forming firm in order to keep it going. As one GP put it, "You can be $100 million down before you realize you've hired a bad partner."

With such small groups, moreover, a dominant GP could turn the partnership into, in effect, a committee of one—raising the chances of bad investments. A pair of dominant founders could be selfish in their allocation of returns, especially to younger professionals, starv-ing a fund of new blood and imperiling long-term success.

All of these problems occur under conditions of extreme uncer-tainty. Before attempting drastic action, VC firms need to some-how evaluate whether present-day difficulties are simply the teeth-ing troubles of a young investee on its way toward future success or whether they are the early signs of a mistake. When seeking to cor-rect a mistake, VC firms need to somehow become confident that they are not abandoning a potential "home run."

Overall, VC firms face in-formation and collective-action problems in ways resembling those of government agencies seeking flexibility in managing portfolios of public programs.

VC firms face information and collective-action problems similar to government agencies seeking flexibility in managing portfolios of public programs

From this perspective, the analytical framework described above can be applied to VC firms as follows: "Structural features" refer to the relationships and incentives between LPs and GPs and between GPs and investees; "formal techniques" refer to written processes with-in VC firms such as standard procedures, formal evaluation criteria, and formal decision-making criteria; and "informal techniques" refer to firms' "unwritten way of doing things."[9]

Structural Features

The dominant structural fact for VC firms is that, in five-to-ten years, the GPs will have to raise one or more new funds or the firm is literally out of business.

Firms differ in the extent to which GPs are reminded of this. In one case of a failed firm, the dominant GP monopolized LP relationships. Alternatively, in a top-quartile firm, all GPs were reminded of the LPs' expectations for returns at intense annual meetings. A large portion of the LPs in a new fund will often be ones who invested in a prior fund. So, even if these LPs may not withdraw their capital, murmurs of future discontent at annual meetings can spur renewed focus on the part of the GPs even without the LPs being free to micromanage or to reduce flexibility.

Added to this, GPs' personal co-investment and compensation structures create strong medium- and long-term incentives. Typically a firm's GPs and staff will be asked to contribute 1 percent of the capital in a new fund. For individual GPs this can amount to over $1 million in a multibillion-dollar fund. Although most GPs in successful funds have high net worth, and only at the very tail of risk distributions would this capital be lost (as opposed to simply yielding low returns), this remains a substantial investment to put at risk.

In the event of low or negative returns for LPs, the GPs then face professional failure (the firm closing) and substantial personal losses (the opportunity cost on their personal investment). This alignment of medium- and long-term risk creates a level of trust allowing LPs to grant GPs a high degree of discretion, for a decade, in the deployment of their capital.

This is both a freedom and a restriction—as it leaves a mere three-to-five-year timeline for most investments to grow, with only a few lasting marginally longer. Though in the ideal case the structure provides funds great discretion, at times LPs can and do use prospective threats to put pressure on funds to prioritize shorter-term returns.

Relationships are even more complex between VC firms and investees. An investee's management has discretion in its use of capital

—although with less autonomy than if it had not sought and accepted outside funds. Such constraints on management autonomy operate formally through the VC-firm directors' involvement on the investees' company boards.

Informal control actually wielded by VC firms can be much more substantial—particularly if the VC firm has a strong reputation. Investees almost always need to conduct a series of capital raisings as they grow, making them reliant on future investments by their backers. If a VC firm with a strong reputation declines to invest in a subsequent round other potential investors are liable to doubt the investee's viability and may also decline to invest. So VC firms may effectively wield "life or death" power over investees.

Investment agreements will contain provisions stipulating "information rights" or "observer rights" for the VC firm as well as defined investee "milestones" serving to focus activity and may also condition subsequent releases of capital. "Observer rights" are particularly noteworthy since, to some degree, they are contrary to classical contracting theory. Since such rights do not require active performance, they may be legally unenforceable. As such these rights are similar to governance provisions found in the "innovation contracts" whose use in recent years has been growing in the private sector (Gilson, Sabel, and Scott 2009).

In return for their influence and potential intrusion, VC firms provide, at least in theory, investees with more than financial capital. Often referred to as "value add," VC firms may offer advice and access to networks of customers, employees, and suppliers. VC partners are, however, far from omniscient and vary in quality, so such advice may not only be of poor quality, it may even actually destroy an investee. By the time such advice is offered, partners from the VC firm may already be on the board of the investee, leaving the investee in a poor position to resist.

Industry observers and participants often cite the quality of a VC firm's networks (even more than its advice) as among the most significant factors in relative VC firm performance. Firms known for strong value add will tend to have the best start-ups seeking their investment and will obtain the best terms for their investment. VC firms with a history of offering the wrong type of value add to the wrong sector or stage of investee growth, or that just have frequently given bad advice, are liable to have to chase deals or invest on poor terms. Investees themselves are, after all, taking a risk on the quality of the VC GPs when they accept funding. These risks are informally priced through the different deal terms offered to different prospective investors.[10]

With these interlocking incentives and instruments, VC firms may place far more trust in an investee than other financial institutions might. VC firms gain access to information and influence over management in excess of typical minority shareholders. This is as important—if not more so—than hierarchy and legal rules, which were rarely mentioned in interviews.

Finally, there is the landscape beyond the investees. As Janeway (2012) argues, VC firms require a highly liquid equity market prone to bouts of speculative excess or regulatory structures creating huge rents at well-defined stages of development. Either or both periodically offer valuations that create "home runs." This search for "speculative excess" is arguably what has driven so much venture capital to information technology (IT) and biotech and depressed it in clean technology.[11]

More than this, though, as one GP described it, VC firms require "a huge amount of social infrastructure" to be viable. Beyond the standard elements of the business environment, such as infrastructure and regulation, they require a supply of capabilities, and networks between those capabilities, to be able to find and improve the firms in which they invest.[12]

Formal and Informal Techniques

Personnel. Leaving aside LPs, it is instructive to concentrate on the formal processes and structures within VC firms and between VC funds and investees. While LBO funds tend to draw people from finance, venture capital funds tend to draw people from operations. GPs tend to be former senior executives or entrepreneurs. This makes them credible sources of advice to entrepreneurs and often means they have greater experience in judging people's capabilities.

This preference is not rigid. High-quality GPs are considered such a scarce resource, and thus so important to fund performance, that *a priori* rules would constitute a competitive handicap. VC firms, instead, conduct extensive and rigorous screening of potential new

GPs. One fund reported that its LPs would even do the same, compiling deep background reports on a fund's new partners, sometimes through specialist investigators.

Interviewees resisted providing any hard-and-fast rules for the screening process and selection criteria other than general characteristics ("judgment" being cited most often). Founders or senior executives of a start-up, which later became a "home run," once funded by a VC firm, were considered to be particularly strong candidates. Even such strong candidates, though, were not believed risk-free and would not be spared the rigorous screening applied to candidates with less attractive backgrounds.

Typical VC firms have five-to-seven GPs. Even the largest of VC firms have no more than thirty "partners" and fewer still "general partners." Several interviewees stated that they thought a firm with more than five or ten GPs simply would not work. Even those firms that have grown larger seem to have done so by grouping *de facto* distinct funds under a single brand name.[13] GPs and observers concurred that the primary constraint on GP numbers within a fund is the quality of decision-making. With more GPs, information flow is impeded, common knowledge is harder to create, and group dynamics become more difficult to manage.[14]

Information. Most VC firms hold two kinds of formal meetings.

Weekly meetings, usually held on Mondays, have each GP discussing one or two of his or her investees—focusing on those soon to need financing, exit, or major changes to the management team or business conditions. These weekly meetings are considered a core operating process and are not missed by GPs other than for exceptional circumstances.

Quarterly, semi-annually, or annually, VC firms conduct exhaustive reviews (although time devoted to each specific investment will vary substantially) of every investee within their portfolios.

Both types of meetings only provide the "bones" for a much larger body of information—informal channels provide the "flesh."

Partners gather as much information as possible on the performance of each of their investees. Some information is gathered formally through board meetings, reporting requirements, and information-rights provisions.

The bulk of the information generation that informs management decisions, though, comes from informal communications. At least once a week, GPs—or the investment professionals on their team—call, e-mail, or visit 80–90 percent of their investees' CEOs and other senior managers (Waldeck, Wainwright, and Blaydon 2003). They probe for additional management insights and offer executives the opportunity to ask questions.

The bulk of the information generation that informs management decisions, though, comes from informal communications

GPs tend to limit their formal time commitments, preferring to avoid chairing company boards. Prospective time requirements from GPs are often included in their evaluation of potential investees (Kaplan and Strömberg 2000b). Some funds ration time, and develop younger talent, by insisting on observer rights for younger staff. Such assignments also provide younger staff invaluable education.

Within VC firms, GPs generally speak with each other frequently, well beyond the extent of their weekly meeting. Firms have failed when one GP became dominant, reducing information flow, and the dominant partner made misguided decisions his or her peers were unable to mitigate.[15]

Information-flow content is adjusted with time and performance (Waldeck, Wainwright, and Blaydon 2003). Staff working with a GP will use whatever information may be important at that moment to continually frame hypotheses regarding current and future performance—testing these ideas against market scenarios and subjecting these ideas to fierce debate and judgment within the team.

The most common metric across all stages is cash. Meanings given this metric, though, may vary. VC firms may consider excessive "cash burn" (spending) a positive factor, demonstrating proactive management. Viewed by a different firm—or even the same firm monitoring a different investee—excessive cash burn may be believed to signify a lack of fiscal discipline. Similarly, lower-than-expected cash burn may reflect prudence, turbulence, or execution problems. So cash burn and other metrics are used to identify trends, to generate opinions, and to trigger decisions.

The most important of these opinions concerns management. In a review of fund investments, investees with management teams rated "strong" at the initial evaluation were three times as likely to later go public as those with management teams initially rated "weak."

The attractiveness of the investees' market made no comparable difference. VC firms expect to intervene to shape the management team in more than half of their investments (Kaplan and Strömberg 2000b). Hence the information flow is focused on the management team and on its interaction with customers, employees, and suppliers. Cash and other metrics are tools to bring information concerning the management team to the surface and these metrics are rarely judged in isolation.

Decision-making. Assessments of both personnel and information lead to decision-making. Simplifying somewhat, there are two primary VC-firm decisions: initially whether to financially support a possible investee and then, triggered either by the need for a new series of fund-raising or by investee problems, whether to continue with an investment or exit.

Multiple models, ranging from requiring a "consensus" to requiring a formal majority vote, exist for making the first decision.[16]

A GP who had been involved in multiple funds reported that the most common way for an investment to be approved was if most partners were in favor, if no more than one or two were opposed, and if the opposition of those opposed was cautionary rather than adamant. Most interviewees reported that, prior to a new commitment of capital, every partner must have the opportunity to see and vet the investment proposal.

In effect this creates a committee structure with a variable but relatively high degree of consensus required to approve decisions. Such a structure guards carefully against "type II" errors, i.e., investing in bad prospects (Sah and Stiglitz 1988).

The second decision, if it needs to be made, is arguably more difficult.[17] Processes for such decisions vary widely and often rely on highly informal practices among the GPs. Three practices seem to be common in many such decisions. First, the decision is, above all, prospective, or forward-looking, avoiding the "sunk cost" fallacy. Second, the decision concentrates on problem-solving, particularly with and about the management team. Third, when it results in termination, the decision-making process itself reduces intangible exit costs.

The first of those practices is clearly easier said than done. A useful technique, as one GP described it, is to ask: "What will it take for us to make five times our money on this firm?" The question forces VC-firm staff to make simple calculations, such as the required market size and share, and then to probe if these conditions remain plausible. Staff consider the investment required to meet these conditions, both in cash and in their own time and effort, and estimate what such an investment might alternatively yield in other options within their portfolios. These tests focus on the key financial issues and on whether or not home runs remain feasible. Such tests enforce clarity in the thinking of VC firms.

The second practice relies on the question, "What can we fix?" In more detail:

- Do we still believe in this management team? If not, is it a problem of a limited number of individuals or is it most of the team? Do we have the weight on the board to initiate changes?
- If we initiate management changes, are we confident a new or reshuffled team will set the firm right or will we have to step into the breach ourselves? What else could our GPs be doing with that amount of time?
- If we believe in the management team, are the problems they face ones we know about? Can we provide them with technical or managerial expertise to fix these problems?
- Can we provide introductions to new partners, new customers, new employees, or new suppliers? Are they missing some piece of the network they need to succeed, possibly a piece we have?

Such decisions will vary in quality depending on the depth of understanding the VC firm has regarding its investee. When asked how his firm decided on exit, one interviewee answered that such decisions are made through the depth and quality of the firm's interaction with the investee. The same criteria applies to the ability to execute remedial actions. While some firms, as described previously, may hold substantial informal power over investees, using this power is likely to damage investee-management morale at a time of acute vulnerability.

This is not to say funds will not resort to command-and-control—but this is considered a last resort and can be seen as a failure. As one interviewee put it, "You only resort to authority when your brains have failed."

If the above questions are exhausted without finding "something to fix," exit begins, emphasizing the importance of the third practice noted above. By this point the investee situation should be common knowledge within the VC firm. Social costs among GPs will have been taken in regular, small doses at weekly meetings and in informal discussions. Avoiding dwelling on sunk costs will tend to minimize the assigning of "blame." If one or more GPs still resist accepting the loss, he, she, or they will have little if any information advantage over fellow GPs—making resistance simply on the basis of stubbornness more difficult. Small size, a focus on information, and a clear process of decision-making smooth the costs of admitting failure within VC firms.

Often VC funds will invest alongside other VC funds in the same investee. If these other funds choose not to exit at the same time, the one that does exit may suffer both financial and reputational damage. Practices similar to those used internally help with this problem as well. A GP reported that good funds give each other sufficient signaling so that, by the time an exit occurs, "everyone knows."

Pre-existing reputation, however, seems to be a significant factor. Exit by a VC firm known to "cut and run" is likely to be interpreted as a reflection on the firm's character rather than on the condition of the investee. Exit by a VC firm with a reputation for success will instead concentrate attention on the investee. Given the uncertainties involved in start-ups, reputation is likely as good a basis for screening as the putative quality of technical analyses.

Path-dependence should not be underestimated: prior success can be one of the most important criteria for the future success of a VC firm

This observation prompts a cautionary note on path-dependence. Multiple interviewees held that prior success is one, and perhaps the most important, criterion for the future success of a VC firm. Causation likely flows in both directions since prior success, dependent on both capabilities and luck, builds social and reputational capital which creates further capabilities and an often-self-fulfilling belief in "luck." This puts a significant premium on the mistakes or successes of earlier years.

Summary

An interlocking set of characteristics and techniques allows VC funds to overcome, in part, the issues of uncertainty, adaptive management, and exit costs.

Uncertainty can be divided into two phases: first, the initial investment decision, and, second, decisions to maintain investment when an investee is struggling or to increase investment in one that is promising. The first phase is weighted toward avoiding bad investments, and therefore relies on consensus; the second phase is weighted toward avoiding missed opportunities, and therefore relies on autonomy. Both phases employ a mix of quantitative and qualitative information, using rigorous evaluation but few strict rules. Both prioritize judgments about the capabilities of the investee management team.

To improve the odds of the success of their investment post-decision, VC firms emphasize thick information flows and working closely with the investee management team. In pursuing these approaches, VC firms focus on "value add": the customers, employees, suppliers, executives, and ideas that VC firms may bring to an investee to make the investee more likely to succeed. GPs are often chosen for their "value add" and junior staff are often evaluated on their maturity and restraint in dealing with entrepreneurs.

Thick flows of information then reduce some of the intangible costs of exit from failure—which happens only when other responses are exhausted or when those responses are too costly and the chance of hitting a home run is assessed as remote.

Undergirding these techniques is the size and clarity of long-term incentives. If the fund fails, the GP loses substantial wealth and, perhaps, his or her career. This allows LPs to grant (albeit while maintaining continuous pressure) VC firms flexibility in deploying capital and mitigates the risk of VC firms becoming emotionally captured by their investments.[18] It concentrates organizational focus forward rather than backward and prevents information flow from becoming mere talk.

Long-term discipline, existential but suspended, allows short-term flexibility, realized through small groups wrapped in thick information flows focusing on capabilities and networks. While too many early mistakes may be fatal, early successes may snowball—creating organizations sometimes helping change the world and providing their principals and agents enormous returns.

The Curious Case of DARPA

Many interviewees said that the flexibility of venture capitalists would be "impossible" at a larger scale—or at any agency within government. One remarkable case indicates otherwise, however, since it occurs in a setting both large and public. By the accounts of many, venture capital's best-known successes would have been impossible without it.[19]

The Defense Advanced Research Projects Agency, better known as DARPA, was created in 1958 in the US Department of Defense (DoD) as part of the US response to the perceived technological threat illustrated by the Soviet Union's launch of the satellite Sputnik. DARPA's explicit mission was "to prevent technological surprise." The cast of the mission has changed over the years but, throughout, DARPA has always addressed big problems demanding big solutions (Fuchs 2010).

DARPA was born into an institutional landscape already including multiple government agencies funding research. These ranged from various research and development (R&D) offices in the military services (e.g., in aviation development) to specialized agencies (e.g., the Atomic Energy Commission) to the broadly mandated National Science Foundation. Military and intelligence services were particularly active in research in areas from funding the development of the U2 spy-plane to atomic energy (Bennis and Biederman 1997; Ruttan 2006). In the wake of Sputnik, DARPA was created to remedy what were seen as two flaws in this architecture: the silo mentality of the services (Carleton 2010) and the perceived conservatism in agencies such as the NSF (Piore 2011).

In pursuing its mandate DARPA embodies flexibility, accepting success-failure ratios comparable to those of the riskiest VC firms (Dugan 2012). DARPA's track record is staggering—from seeding the Internet to creating stealth and global positioning system (GPS) technologies to maintaining the United States' lead in semiconductors. It is public, ten times the size of a typical VC firm, and is both flexible and effective.

Description

DARPA has historically had a budget of approximately $3 billion per year. It operates slightly outside the civil-service hiring process and standard government contracting rules but it remains within the basic parameters of the Department of Defense (Bonvillian 2006) under the Office of the Secretary of Defense.[20]

DARPA is currently divided into six "offices," each with an office director (OD).[21] Its work is organized into programs which last for roughly four years—although larger and more complex programs can extend over multiple cycles (Bonvillian and Van Atta 2011). Around 25 percent of DARPA's budget, or about $750 million, becomes available each year as programs end. That sum is called "the wedge." This amount is allocated, in part to existing programs but primarily to new ones, either by the director of DARPA or by the office directors.[22]

Programs are the core of DARPA and each program is expected to embody a "technological vision" (Carleton 2010). Within each program, almost all decisions are made by the program manager (PM). For most of DARPA's existence, there have been 100–150 PMs, almost all serving for no more than four years.

For most of its functions other than program management, DARPA uses administrative, contracting, and technical services from other agencies or private-sector firms (Piore 2011). This provides DARPA the flexibility to get in and out of programs without the burden of sustaining staff. Since support firms frequently conduct repeat work with the agency, these support firms serve as carriers of organizational knowledge—including how to navigate the system surrounding DARPA.

DARPA's success has led to many attempts at replication. Two prominent recent examples have been in energy (Advanced Research Projects Agency-Energy [ARPA-E]) and intelligence (Intelligence Advanced Research Projects Activity [IARPA]). As each is less than a decade old, it is far too early to fully evaluate either. ARPA-E, however, seems to have embodied many of DARPA's features more successfully than prior attempts at "DARPA clones" (Bonvillian and Van Atta 2011).

As it did not attempt a full study of venture capital firms, this paper does not seek to provide a complete study of DARPA.[23] This paper only seeks to review how, operating at an extreme edge of uncertainty and within a military bureaucracy, DARPA manages to pursue multiple approaches while knowing many will fail.

The focus will be on the structures, rules, and informal processes through which DARPA has implemented flexibly—in particular those features which seem to have remained common through its changes over the years. As DARPA will be analyzed using the same framework previously applied to the VC industry, this study will draw contrasts where applicable. These insights have been drawn from interviews with former DARPA management, PMs, and outside researchers who have studied the organization. As with VC firms, recipients of DARPA funds have not been interviewed.

> *From its early years, DARPA's mission was to prevent Soviet technological surprises and, by the 1970s and early/mid 1980s to, in some fashion, nullify Soviet military capabilities*

Structural Features

DARPA's relationship to its primary client, broadly described as the US defense complex, is among its most important structural features and has had multiple effects. DARPA exhibited an early clarity in recognizing its long-term mission, which was seen as directly linked to the threats faced by the US military. In its initial years, primary threats were perceived to be Soviet technological surprises—and DARPA's mission was to prevent such surprises. Examples include predominating in space exploration and use, detecting nuclear tests, and creating a resilient information network.

In the 1970s and early/mid 1980s, the threat was then-existing Soviet military capabilities. DARPA's mission was to, in some fashion, nullify these capabilities. Stealth technologies, precision-strike weaponry, and other components of the "revolution in military affairs" followed (Van Atta 2013).

As military threats evolved, and for a brief period became insignificant, DARPA's mission also evolved (Fuchs 2010). With the end of the Cold War the agency had less clarity in its mission. In the late 1980s and the 1990s greater emphasis was first laid on "dual use" technology applications and then, more broadly, on general US industrial competitiveness. Some have seen this as an evolution and maturation in US industrial policy (Fong 2000). Most of those interviewed, though, characterized this time as a period of drift, and a period of incremental advances on past glories.

Though this should not be overstated, given the range of tangible advances in high-tech industries in the 1990s and that radical advances require decades to be visible, questions about the continued effectiveness of the agency are much less easily dismissed now than they may have been two decades ago.

Thus it is worth considering the features of DARPA's mission, particularly during its early decades when it achieved its most notable successes, in more depth. Both "avoiding technological surprise" and "nullifying Soviet military capabilities" share these features:

- *Little ambiguity in measurement.* Both goals have only one variable (have we been surprised? are Soviet military capabilities nullified?), which is a binary, "yes/no," question.
- *Much ambiguity in attribution.* Whether the result could have happened without DARPA is impossible (at least to the level of an academic evaluation) to answer.
- *Clear consequences for failure.* It is straightforward to answer, "What happens if this is not achieved?" The United States would have been potentially vulnerable to attack and might have been at risk of losing the Cold War.
- *Political consequences for failure.* Members of the political elite would feel threatened, personally and politically, by such failure or by any perception of having individually contributed to such failure.
- *Extreme ambition.* For the United States to *never* be surprised and to *fully nullify* its adversary's military capabilities the United States must be the home of *all* salient breakthroughs.

These characteristics of the description of DARPA's mission had multiple enabling effects.

First, clarity of measurement disciplined flexibility by making it hard to fudge the question of how, whether as a putative success or as a potential failure, a program answered the overall mission. It is much easier, for example, to fudge an answer to, "How does this improve US competitiveness?" than, "Which Soviet military capability will this nullify?"

Second, the clarity and consequences of failure made opposition difficult in the short term, giving the agency political space, and later made opposition impossible once DARPA had established a track record of success. It also meant the agency faced a highly credible threat of its own demise if it did fail because political pressure would be intense to reform or remove it. That meant the definition of the agency's mission had to answer a threat credibly framed and accepted as vital by the political elite. The framing of such a threat requires considerable rhetorical skill and an absence of wishful thinking.

Third, the ambition of the goal serves to create both short-term space and long-term discipline. In the short term it means the agency can use the enormity of the task to justify major risks, even "unreasonable" ones, as well as failures. In the long term it means that whether or not the goal has been met will be obvious and that it cannot be hidden or waved away. Small goals are liable to be forgotten, allowing a failing agency to hope its failure would not be noticed or that a few partial successes might rescue it.

In sum, in an idealized form, clear and simple long-term goals liberated short-term programs from incrementalism; a present threat created the political space for the unusual and for potential failure. Clarity disciplined flexibility by making it hard to fudge the question of how a program answers the overall mission.

In addition to its mission, the system of institutions within which DARPA operates is the other structural feature vital to the agency's effectiveness. The agency neither conducts research itself nor implements any of its programs. DARPA is explicitly and continuously oriented towards a network of customers (both military and civilian), firms, and researchers and it plays an active role in maintaining and expanding that network through formal and informal means. DARPA funds researchers—within academic or commercial institutions, large and small—and connects them and their output to implementers or customers.[24] It is inherently an intermediary so it requires other agents among which it can intermediate.

Many of the techniques DARPA employs thus depend on access to an exceptionally diverse range of capabilities. The problem that DARPA solves is one of capabilities: that of finding, connecting, and funding a combination of firms and individuals who can together generate and implement a technical solution. As such, the more diverse the supply of such capabilities on which it can draw, the more effective it can be.

DARPA is not passive with regards to this network and actively shapes it. DARPA does so within programs (Fuchs 2010) or across strategic thrusts (Bonvillian and Van Atta 2011). At times it even architects its own structural features by consciously creating new networks.

The most striking case of this is the network of laboratories and companies now dominating high-tech research. To a large extent this network is the creation of DARPA's early years, when it set out not only to attack the computing dominance of IBM (International Business Machines Corporation) but to create new faculties and laboratories from Stanford to Utah to MIT (Massachusetts Institute of Technology) and, indirectly, to Xerox PARC (Palo Alto Research Center) itself (Fong 2001). Finding no network, DARPA seeded one.

The importance of the combination of DARPA's mission outlook and its network orientation will be a theme throughout the discussion of its formal and informal features. Reflecting their importance, flawed missions or flawed client relationships have sometimes been described as key weaknesses in attempts to replicate DARPA.

As the most notable example, while ARPA-E has attained significant technical capabilities, and adopted a similar and explicit orientation towards building and maintaining its surrounding system (Bonvillian and Van Atta 2011), its mission is a cause for potential concern. The ARPA-E mission has been variously described as "advancing high-potential, high-impact technologies that are too early for private-sector investment," or "[solving] energy challenges that could radically improve U.S. economic prosperity, national security and environmental well-being." This is quite distant from, for example, "achieve zero carbon," or "end fossil-fuel imports" (as illustrative equivalents, in this field, of DARPA's earlier missions).

Some have expressed concerns that ARPA-E's outlook is incremental, arguably reflected by the large number of applications it receives (i.e., it may be that too many organizations can address the limited goals ARPA-E defines). ARPA-E has, however, evolved techniques to address this concern and it may yet evolve a more radical informal understanding of its mission.

Formal Techniques

Personnel. DARPA PMs' backgrounds are eclectic—they arrive from academia, government, and industry. At a more specific level there are few clear patterns—PMs come from and go to jobs in almost every field and activity.[25] Over the decades their age seems to be increasing (Carleton 2010). They share a common sense that working at DARPA is "the most exciting thing they will ever do" and are considered visionaries (ibid.). Colloquially they are characterized as "freewheeling zealots with balls and brains" (Dugan 2012).

These descriptions are supported by one of DARPA's most striking organizational features: strict term limits for PMs. PMs serve for one term of up to four years, formally divided into a first two years and then a one-time-only two-year renewal. There are seldom any renewals beyond this unless a PM becomes an office director. This happens for, at most, about 5 percent of PMs.

This policy of strict term limits produces wide-ranging effects.

First, term limits curb vested interests within the agency, although they do not fully eliminate informal fiefs. Directors, however, can remove such fiefs, should they wish to, through their power of appointment of PMs and the turnover of directors has largely been similarly rapid (with the exception of Tony Tether staying 2001–2009; Fuchs 2010).

Second, term limits screen the personality types of DARPA PMs. Agreeing to become a PM is a substantial risk. In mid-career an individual must leave what is often secure employment for a four-year opportunity with nothing definite at the end. Would-be PMs must believe that, within those four years, they can achieve enough so that, when their four years are completed, they will easily find a much better job than that which they

Term limits curb vested interests within the agency, screen the personality types of DARPA PMs, and help to create loyalty

left. Leaving aside, for the moment, the risk of collusion (which will be treated later in this paper), this means that, by self-selection, PMs cannot be risk-averse (Carleton 2010).

Third, term limits create loyalty. PMs must be willing to relocate for four years. Because early exits from DARPA are unusual, after they have joined DARPA an early exit would send a strong negative signal to potential future employers. Becoming a PM thus has high entry and exit costs, which can be expected to foster loyalty (Hirschman 1970).

In sum, if collusion risk is contained, the four-year rule creates in PMs a cadre of risk-tolerant, loyal, technical experts with an ethos and high personal incentives to achieve substantial results in a short timeframe. It should be noted, however, that such techniques on their own will not automatically generate DARPA-like results or even DARPA-like PMs.[26]

Decision-making. DARPA's basic decision-making architecture is flat, rapid, and, once programs are approved, provides even more autonomy than VC funds.

Programs must be approved by the office director and then by the DARPA director. Programs are subject to witheringly intense reviews attended by other ODs and multiple PMs. Often there is a further layer of informal scrutiny: that of the Office of the Secretary of Defense and—formerly—that of the Director of Defense Research and Engineering (DoD).

While the DARPA director has the ultimate say, a near-consensus is often implicitly required for a program's approval. This combination of hierarchical and collective decision-making can be expected to cut down on "type II" errors—the approval of bad programs. Once programs are approved, however, PMs usually have substantial autonomy. Such autonomy can then be expected to cut down on "type I" errors—failing to invest in good opportunities.

Three factors play important, varying, and, at times, controversial roles in DARPA decision-making.

The first factor is "vision" (Carleton 2010). To be approved, a new program should aim at a radical innovation (i.e., an entirely new capability). It must have a challenging-but-plausible path to a solution, a path that could not be traversed without DARPA's involvement. In some cases a new PM may already possess this vision—but often it results from a set of formal and informal processes for gathering and connecting ideas from DARPA's networks (ibid.; Fuchs 2010).

The second factor is that of long-term strategic thrusts (Bonvillian and Van Atta 2011). These are not formally laid down but can acquire informal status as the result of a particularly strong long-term vision by a director combined with a bottom-up aggregation of a range of similar programs developing organic relationships to each other.

Once a thrust is present, it eases the approval of any subsequent program fitting within it. The most notable example was information technology, which encapsulates the risks and rewards of such thrusts. Over several decades information technology produced, arguably, DARPA's greatest successes. At the same time DARPA's commitment to information technology may have inhibited the organization's flexibility (when the thrust was eventually curtailed in the 2000s it created an outcry).

The third factor, and a point of particular controversy, is the importance of a "customer": a military service or, on occasion, a civilian sector committed to implementing solutions once DARPA has brought them far enough along.

Once the services are convinced that they are capable of almost single-handedly implementing a new technology, they can and often will provide political cover for its development. PMs may find, within the same institutional umbrella, a "customer" able to both protect and implement the program.

Alternatively, this need for a "customer" sometimes becomes a screening device. In doing so it may provide discipline but may also block creativity, particularly if the program wishes to tackle a challenge so difficult that its solution cannot yet even be outlined.

Adding such a test implicitly adds a level of hierarchy to program approval, shifting the balance of risk toward rejecting good programs and away from approving a bad ones. In striking that balance, directors' estimates of which risk is more serious probably influences the degree to which they impose such a test—in itself, this is perhaps a judgment of whether the agency's culture at the time is thought to be too permissive or too conservative.[27]

These three factors, within the context of the structural conditions described above, produce a delicate balance of creativity and discipline. The emphasis on vision enables the pursuit of radical innovation which alone can meet the demanding mission. Balancing this there is a risk that, as former German Chancellor Helmut Schmidt once said, "people who have visions should go see a doctor."

Constraints seeming to keep DARPA's visions healthy are the simplicity of the mission; requiring strategic thrusts to be validated by bottom-up successes in programs; the aggregation of "visions" from interactions and connections among DARPA's network of the best minds in their fields; and, when it is used, the customer-demand test.

This delicate balance is perhaps best articulated in the "Heilmeier Catechism," consisting of the following series of questions:[28]

- What are you trying to do? Articulate your objectives using absolutely no jargon.
- How is it done today, and what are the limits of current practice?
- What's new in your approach and why do you think it will be successful?
- Who cares? If you're successful, what difference will it make?
- What are the risks and the payoffs?
- How much will it cost? How long will it take?
- What are the "midterm exams" and "final exams" to check for success?

Every program must be able to answer these questions at approval and in reviews thereafter. The catechism connects DARPA's mission to decision-making at the level of programs, using repeated interrogations to link the organization and progress of specific initiatives to the agency's mission to generate technological breakthroughs.

Program Management. Once a program is approved, the PM's task is to assemble, monitor, and manage research projects undertaking different approaches to achieving a technological breakthrough. These are detailed in contracts specifying recipients, the approaches they will take, the milestones and targets for the research, and the funding that DARPA will provide.

During most of DARPA's existence, PMs have retained a high degree of autonomy in writing programs' contracts (the possible exception being the 2001–2009 tenure of Tony Tether, though the extent of any change is the subject of fierce debate). DARPA does not conduct peer review. While PMs can submit contracts for review by external experts, they seldom do so—and, when they do, they are not bound by the results.[29]

Nevertheless, PMs are subject to regular progress reviews throughout the life of their program. A principal tool for evaluation is the repeated informal application of the Heilmeier Catechism. As such it is useful to consider in more detail the structure of this "catechism."

Its emphasis is first on the idea itself and its degree of innovation, then on the arrangements and process for generating results, and then on the definition of intermediate results. Their sequence and hierarchy is important. The difficulty of the problem comes first, then the innovative idea, then the impact.

Organizational arrangements precede intermediate goals rather than follow them. Questions five and six are phrased in terms of "how" more than "what": "How will results be generated?" not "What will the results be?"—and "How will you measure progress?" not "What will you measure?"

DARPA's evaluation routine is thus more focused on tangible and substantial progress in solving difficult problems and less focused on hitting quantified targets. Although DARPA's results on metrics, such as patents per dollar of funding, far outstrip those of most other agencies, insiders will refuse to even admit such metrics as valid indicators of their performance.[30]

> *DARPA is more focused on tangible and substantial progress in solving difficult problems and less focused on hitting quantified targets*

Even when DARPA, in the last decade, came closest to traditional results-management, with the director requiring formal progress milestones and threatening projects' cancellation if they were not met, in practice this threat was seldom carried out. Yet it seems telling that this period evoked strong and often diametrically opposing views from interviewees. Some characterized it as a "trauma" requiring "a long time to heal." Others argued with equal vehemence such management was necessary for an agency drifting aimlessly with a rising failure rate and a necessary response to the changing structure of the system surrounding DARPA. [31]

Overall the agency seems to follow a path between the extremes of close monitoring of fixed targets and complete autonomy with fuzzy goals. One way to encapsulate this is "judgment-based management founded on performance metrics." PMs use this concept in managing contracts much as ODs and directors use it in managing programs.[32]

In reality this may be easier said than done and seems related to DARPA's mission. DARPA's orientation toward breakthroughs militates against close monitoring and fixed targets; but a sense of existential threat, and the pressing needs of a demanding mission, prevent too much drift. Thus the loss of clarity following the Cold War led the agency to veer off this middle path in both directions. Operationally, this observation reinforces clarity of measurement ("Has there been an important breakthrough?") over clarity of attribution ("Would it have happened without you?").

Informal Techniques

Contract Management. DARPA contracts are informally known to have impossible performance goals.[33]

At first glance this might seem to compromise accountability but, in practice, setting such goals serves two functions. First, such goals trigger continuous discussion and problem-solving as formal goals are frequently unmet. Second, such goals create a continual justification for PMs to intervene, should they wish to, in the workings of the contract.

In a sense, such goals are like VC "observer rights" provisions or extreme precursors of "innovation contracts" (Gilson, Sabel, and Scott 2009), just as they are natural offshoots of the long-standing Department of Defense commitment to open information sharing and diffusion (Ruttan 2006; Janeway 2012).

Contract management, then, focuses on the firm's or consortium's capabilities and knowledge networks.

When a contract seems to be in difficulty the first response is to introduce a new source of knowledge or to restructure the team, often in workshops described as "no holds barred."[34] PMs require different parties, who together may have the capabilities required to solve the problem, to come together and tell each other about what they are doing.

An alternative response is to reassess if the contractor might still achieve some breakthrough, albeit perhaps not its original goal.

This process is sometimes described as "spending all the time talking"—but this is purposeful, active talking. PMs, in this respect, are facilitators. They don't just award a contract, go away, and wait for outcomes: They take active roles in discussing progress with their contractors and defining results.[35] They are held more accountable for not knowing *why* a program is having trouble—not having enough information about what is going wrong and potential solutions—than for the trouble *per se.*

Initial stages of programs are often heavily focused on establishing needed information flows. PMs initially spend large amounts of their time studying relevant fields of knowledge and speaking to researchers. PMs conduct seminars bringing together people who would otherwise rarely or never talk with each other (Fuchs 2010). Once they acquire some degree of mastery of the fields of knowledge related to their program, PMs create broad agency announcements (BAAs) or requests for proposals (RFPs) leading to contracts. Winning bids on those BAAs or RFPs are then selected on the basis of the capabilities of the firm or consortium as much as on the basis of the approach. Formal and frequent contract-review meetings take place. As with VC firms, these meetings establish a regular rhythm amid the continuous process of informal information-sharing.

Failure Tactics. It is often said that DARPA has a unique ability to fail and survive because of its position within the military. This case is less robust than it appears. Many public programs survive, despite repeated failures, through bureaucratic inertia or interest-group lobbying. The military is no exception. So what is interesting is not DARPA's ability to fail, but its ability to admit failure and redirect resources away from it.

In this regard, DARPA should face many of the constraints others do. Its funding creates interests, namely recipients, who would be hurt by cancellations. Many of these recipients, often defense contractors, are exceptionally effective lobbyists (Mothershed 2011). Former PMs reported it was not unusual to be summoned by politicians demanding funding be restored or a program extended to include a firm with operations in the politician's constituency.

DARPA is also surrounded by agencies that could be expected to compete with DARPA for budget resources.[36] Outside the military, that includes the networks of research laboratories and science foundations; within the military, that includes the services' own laboratories and R&D programs. These rivals might be eager to seize on admitted failures as a means to capture DARPA's funding. Overall, DARPA faces obstacles to admitting failure that are familiar to other areas of bureaucratic life, especially those often articulated for development aid (Gibson et al. 2005).

Several resources help DARPA overcome those obstacles.

The first is simply its track record. Decades of success have created enormous stocks of political capital. The agency's well-developed reputation gives DARPA the day-to-day power to resist a great deal of bureaucratic rivalry and lobbying.

The second resource is the separation of programs and approaches. This allows DARPA to argue that, even if some of its approaches fail, its programs do not. Even where programs, as a whole, are in trouble, they can be and often are substantially reoriented to achieve new purposes—as long as those new purposes still solve big, measurable problems. The more rigorous screening of programs, rather than approaches, also reduces the chances of outright failures at the program level.

The third resource is the fact that DARPA does not engage in direct research itself but funds others to do the research. By that process, it co-opts potential opponents. The larger a contractor, the more likely that contractor is to be involved in multiple contracts from multiple programs. The loss a contractor might suffer from the cancellation of a single contract may thus be mitigated by gains elsewhere and, if a contractor took a confrontational strategy toward DARPA, it would surely create substantial risks to other contracts, present and future.

DARPA's fourth and final resource is the array of side-effects of some of its daily working methods. DARPA's outreach to the military services creates, while programs are under way, protectors and champions with substantial political capital. By bringing to the surface large volumes of information, exhausting options before termination, and engaging in continual discussion, it often generates implicit cover before a decision and helps contain the cost of delays resulting from failed contracts. And, by explicitly targeting radical change, there is an inherent rationale when a given approach fails to succeed.

Collusion and Capture. One might also expect DARPA to face informal risks to its effectiveness due to informal collusion and capture.[37] Such a concern would be particularly acute for any attempt to replicate the agency in an environment of poor governance. As one example, PMs could respond to their limited terms by channeling contracts to companies or institutions in anticipation of, or in exchange for, lucrative employment after they leave the agency. A similar opportunity could arise in favoring companies or institutions in battles among different contractors for patent rights.

DARPA maintains various formal rules to restrict these and similar possible abuses. In January 2013 the DoD's inspector general published a report (Inspector General 2013) finding DARPA complied with these rules. Several interviewees, however, acknowledged that only so much could be done to eliminate the risks. Beyond explicit rules and careful personnel selection, DARPA simply "lives with" the risk.

It may be that a certain level of risk is a necessary consequence of hiring high-quality technical experts for limited periods to oversee programs involving institutions in which they have and will make their careers.

Only a limited number of institutions can perform at the level DARPA requires. Their capabilities stem from the skills of their people and these people will be, by pre-selection, among the very few good enough to become DARPA hires. So the same academic institutions, companies, and laboratories which can and do regularly receive DARPA contract funding are also some of the primary sources supplying DARPA with its PMs.[38] Should DARPA be forced to diversify its contracting from its hiring to reduce the risk of

> *Some collusion risk may be a necessary consequence of hiring experts for limited periods overseeing programs involving institutions in which they have and will make their careers*

collusion, its pool of potential partners and PMs might become less capable. Indeed, some have expressed concern that more restrictive current policies and greater scrutiny are already reducing the quality of PMs.[39]

So the major risk is not that the agency might be captured by the "best of the best," which is effectively the same as the agency simply exercising high-quality selection. The risk, instead, is capture by those who are not the best, leading to a slide into underperformance. One can imagine, particularly in a weak governance environment, a DARPA-like agency becoming a patronage machine with politicians placing clients as PMs—who then lavish funding on underperforming academic institutions, companies, and laboratories for four years after which the PMs exit to high-salaried positions with those they have helped.

The keys to controlling such a scenario are only partially—if at all—"ethics rules" and procurement guidelines. In its glory decades, DARPA's formal controls were far weaker than they are today.

The keys to avoiding such problems, instead, are found in the following:

First—the decision-making and review processes. PMs are given autonomy but must regularly answer the Heilmeier Catechism's demands to show progress toward some breakthrough solution.

Second—the vast exchange of information. This ensures management has low transaction costs in identifying under-performing programs.

Third, and perhaps of most importance—the informal DARPA practice of never relying on any single academic institution, company, or laboratory for too long. While DARPA and MIT, for example, have maintained extremely close ties in IT for many years, DARPA carefully expanded its base over the years well beyond that one institution (and a handful of others) to include a diverse range of IT partnerships.[40]

Although it was difficult to trace such a process in all programs, interviewees suggested it was common practice. When research capabilities were seen as becoming too concentrated, competing relationships would be deliberately fostered—sometimes explicitly—by requiring contractors to host researchers from other organizations as a condition of further funding.[41]

This process, however, might be allowed some lag time. A monopoly on a new set of capabilities might be tolerated, but not for long. Once the first breakthroughs were made the pool of potential new contractors was expected to always be increasing. This links back to DARPA's active management, as described above, of its surrounding system.

The characteristics of DARPA's mission provided a final control. Especially in its early years, the agency was either generating breakthroughs or not—and many in power believed the fate of the country rested on whether it was succeeding. Only in recent decades, after DARPA's original clarity of mission wavered following the end of the Cold War, have formal rules had to be tightened and questions concerning collusion and effectiveness been raised.

Summary

It is worth noting what DARPA does *not* do—as it seems to defy many of the tenets of the literature on public and private management. DARPA does *not* engage in peer review; results measurement; "killing" programs; long-term career development; formal performance incentives; or strict controls against revolving doors, capture, or collusion. This list includes avoiding many of the supposed "best practices" in the folk wisdom of "good governance."

Similarly, DARPA violates several other principles developed in prior work (e.g., Bennis and Biederman 1997) on "innovative organizations." Among these violated principles, though DARPA has had strong directors, it has rarely had leaders of the type described by Bennis and Biederman (1997); it has not declined after the departure of such leaders; it does not work out of physically unattractive surroundings or see itself as an underdog; and, most of all, it is definitively not an "island" (even one with a "bridge") but is deeply embedded in and integrated into its networks.

Yet it is tortuous to construct realistic alternatives which lead, in DARPA's absence, to modern warfare or the information revolution. While DARPA currently seems in decline from its previous dizzying height, the agency still outperforms its peers on measures of basic outcomes. Moreover, without DARPA, several of the "great groups" described in Bennis and Biederman (1997) would not have existed—let alone been able to accomplish what they did.

It is difficult to tease out any single cause for this result since the features described interact so closely with each other. This summary addresses some of the ways in which the identified interactions combine to resolve the problems of flexibility described in the introduction to this paper.

First, *uncertainty*—like VC firms, DARPA distinguishes between the initial investment decision and later actions. The first is subjected to relatively high levels of discipline, to reduce the risk of launching bad programs; later actions are then governed by autonomy.

Second, *the governance and use of discretion*—the mission, as described at length, governs the discretion granted to the agency. With that discretion, DARPA PMs use their incremental funding to manage capabilities. To do so they need a system of diverse capabilities to manage, from public laboratories and defense contractors to individual entrepreneurs and academics. This may sound like a tautology but it is often disregarded in attempts to mimic DARPA.

DARPA, like VC firms, focuses on assembling capabilities and monitoring and acting on thick flows of information. In its programs, as in its mission, DARPA prioritizes measurement over attribution. It uses such measurement only as one tool of management, rather than as a substitute for active management. DARPA's response to potential failure is, likewise, similar to that of VC firms: First, bring more information to the surface; then consider changing the project teams or consortia; then alter goals; and, only as a last resort, consider termination.

Finally, *exit costs*—externally the agency can, and does, claim that "'programs never fail, approaches do." This limits bureaucratic costs by creating defensibility—by allowing failed approaches to, in a sense, hide from the system. This practice provides programs space to potentially morph into a different form of success. Internal costs are limited by the accepted four-year tenure of PMs. If a program is failing, at some point the PM will leave and the sunk costs of personal prestige and attachment will depart with the PM.

DARPA's structural features, however, may be its most important asset. In many ways they make both possible and necessary the techniques described above. DARPA is flexible within and through a system—one that it maintains, cultivates, extends, and monitors. DARPA deploys incremental resources to create or strengthen nodes in this system or to combine nodes. It continually surfaces information from and about this system and recruits from within it.

One effect of this is that DARPA faces an inherent problem of attribution. Another is that DARPA's acting through a system is necessary for the separation of strategic thrusts (shaping the overall structure of the network), programs (deciding to create something new in the network), and approaches (strengthening of individual or combining of nodes).

In symbiosis with this, the measurability, clarity, and politically salient consequences of agency-level failure, translated to program level, mean that repeated failure to exit non-performing approaches would create a highly credible threat of agency termination.

This is strongly reminiscent of the threat faced by VC firms if they do not deliver returns for their limited partners. In both cases it is the existential risk which allows principals to entrust agents with large amounts of discretionary capital; exercise remote monitoring; and allow agents to undertake actions with a high risk of collusion or capture while trusting that these will be controlled so as not to endanger effectiveness. For VC firms the risk is simple and relates to returns. For DARPA the challenge is far from simple. Success depends on the rhetorical skill with which a mission is framed and linked to a threat—which itself is framed to create the widest possible political salience.

Navigating Agencies

Having established some reference parameters with the earlier reviews, this study now turns to its primary focus—discerning patterns and methods of flexibility. How do techniques and characteristics summarized earlier match or contrast with what is known of some famous "navigating agencies" working both in narrowly defined industrial policy and, more broadly, in the process of larger structural transformation?

Some of these agencies were already identified in Table 1: Japan's Ministry of International Trade and Industry (MITI); Korea's Blue House Secretariat; and France's postwar Commissariat General du Plan (CGP). Extensive literature exists on these examples. This study will concentrate on MITI with more limited attention given to the Blue House Secretariat and the CGP.

For contrast, brief attention will be directed to agencies which attempted to deliver flexibility but failed. These include agencies in Kenya, the Philippines, and in the United States under the New Deal.

Given the volume of published prior research, there is difficulty in offering any new observations on MITI. Precisely because it has been so studied, however, over the decades its inner workings have been exposed to both positive and negative scrutiny. This provides useful detail for current purposes.

As with the earlier discussions of VC and DARPA, this study does not seek to provide a thorough new evaluation of MITI or of its role in Japan's achievement of Western income levels.

MITI is examined here principally to understand *how* it did and did not act flexibly in the decades between World War II and the 1990s.

> *MITI is examined principally to understand* how *it did and did not act* flexibly *in the decades between World War II and the 1990s*

That terminal date begs the question of whether and why MITI's flexibility and effectiveness declined as Japan entered its "lost decades." With this consideration, it is worth noting that in the late 1980s and early 1990s Japan and the United States were engaged in direct competition for leadership of the global semiconductor industry. MITI and DARPA played pivotal institutional roles in their respective nations.

Domination of the semiconductor industry was a contest the United States won (among others, see Fuchs 2010). A full accounting of this competition is beyond the scope of this study—though some tentative hypotheses regarding this issue will be offered in closing.

Structural Features

Missions. MITI was driven by Japan's overwhelming post-war social consensus to "catch up," with the clear and simple goal to "double income per capita in a decade." The broad goal of convergence dated from the Meiji era but, in the wake of World War II, it was diverted to focus on technology and applied science rather than military strength (Dower 2000).

This broad consensus was made a sharp goal in successive missions, first for "economic independence" from the United States in the 1950s and then "income doubling" in the 1960s. The latter goal was framed by Prime Minister Ikeda Hayato in 1960, a year of intense political turmoil in Japan when many feared for the survival of the postwar state. The goal was unprecedented in its ambition—and its achievement (indeed, its over-achievement) calmed the political turmoil (Jansen 2009).

MITI's role in the achievement of these goals has been the subject of intense debate. Arguments against MITI's role often deploy sophisticated quantitative techniques (Posen 2002 provides a useful summary). For present purposes the question of attribution is not as important as the internal role these fixed and compelling goals played in disciplining action by MITI officials. Concerning this, the record is relatively clear. The urgent, nationalist, and unambiguous mission and goal continuously disciplined MITI's relationship with the private sector.[42]

Similarly, in Korea, the Blue House Secretariat (in coordination with the Economic Planning Board [EPB]) was dedicated to Park Chung-Hee's vision of "rich country, strong army." This slogan was taken from Meiji-era Japan and was tied directly to national survival: a poor South Korea with a weak army would be acutely vulnerable to North Korea.[43]

In its early years, with the Communist Party attracting a record share of votes in elections and the Cold War beginning, the French CGP had a similarly definitive goal also tied to an immanent threat: to reconstruct and modernize France.

Turning to the cases of failure, Kenya's "Dream Team" in the late 1990s had ambiguous goals: formally, the vague "recovery from crisis"; informally, obtaining donor funds.[44] President Moi's survival depended on keeping his party intact—which required distributing economic rents. "Distributing economic rents" mattered more than reforming government, jobs, growth of gross domestic product, or other such national goals.

Ferdinand Marcos' National Economic Development Agency (NEDA) in the Philippines, ostensibly an attempt to create a navigating agency, had as its goal a "New Society," a vague term inconsequential to the survival of the political elite (Hutchcroft 2011).

The contrast between "unambiguous" and "vague" missions may also hold true when considering some of the "success cases'" later declines to relative stagnation. The CGP declined once the urgent need for reconstruction faded. Korea's Blue House Secretariat declined once Korea had indeed become a rich country with a strong army and a more complex set of goals.[45] MITI's effectiveness declined as Japan reached Western income levels, albeit for a complex set of reasons further discussed below. As Dower (2000) wrote, "while Japan had attained its single-minded goal of 'catching up' to the West economically and technologically, the vision and flexibility necessary for charting a new course were lacking."

Surrounding Systems. Here again there exist some striking similarities. In the years surrounding MITI's creation a wide range of institutions were created or refined. These institutions became the primary channels through which MITI conducted industrial policy.

The best known of these institutions were the advisory councils, under the umbrella of the Industrial Structure Council, which embodied a form of bureau pluralism (Okazaki 2001). These integrated each of MITI's vertical bureaus into large, formal, and complex policy groups.

There was also a panoply of development-finance institutions including the Japan Development Bank and the Fiscal Investment and Loan Plan. Both on their own and through their signaling to the rest of the financial system, these institutions magnified MITI's own resources many-fold—even after MITI lost control of scarce foreign exchange (Johnson 1982). Development of an innovative model of R&D consortia in the 1950s allowed, by the 1970s, public funds in Japan to be leveraged twice as much as in other developed countries (Sakakibara and Cho 2002).

As DARPA was born into an existing research system and then cultivated its growth, and as the stand-out VC firms were born into the results of DARPA's work and then built their own networks for "value add," so MITI inherited a half-formed system from Japan's pre-war and wartime state and then consciously shaped and extended it. At its peak it deployed this system to literally reconstruct global commodity flows—bringing together ports, shipbuilders, steelmakers, utilities, and Japanese export and private banks to render the absence of proximate mineral resources irrelevant to the competitiveness of Japanese heavy industry (Okazaki 2001; Ciccantell and Bunker 2002).

In later decades there seems to have been a subtle shift in MITI's relationship to its surrounding system. In particular, there seems little evidence of institution creation at any level approaching that of the post-war years, with more emphasis on adjusting the scope or powers of the councils and other institutions and instruments. This may, in part, reflect the exhaustion of easy gains and the growth of entrenched interests, most notably in telecommunications, beyond MITI's ability to attack (Okazaki 2001).

In MITI's later years one finds few analogues to DARPA's setting out to create new challengers to IBM or MITI's own earlier 1950s support for the insurgent Kawasaki Steel and its Chiba Works. Rather, the reverse holds, as MITI focused on mergers even after economies of scale were in place (Johnson 1982).

Histories of the Blue House Secretariat and the CGP tell much the same story of the conscious use and tending of surrounding systems (Kim, 2011; Monnet 1978).

Failures, in contrast, often either isolated themselves from or even attacked their relevant systems, as Kenya's "Dream Team" did to that country's civil service. Others kept their coalitions and flows of information narrow, as did the National Recovery Administration in the United States' New Deal whose councils, dominated by the private sector, included little consumer, labor, or public-sector representation (Heinemann 1981).

> *In later decades there seems to have been a subtle shift in MITI's relationship to its surrounding system, with little evidence of the creation of institutions or challengers at the level of the post-war years*

Formal and Informal Techniques

Personnel. MITI, being a cabinet-level ministry of the Japanese government, was far larger than DARPA and certainly far larger than any VC firm. Interviews with former officials indicate that, in its peak years, however, there were only about "a hundred people who mattered."[46] MITI and other successful agencies hired heterogeneously with a bias towards practicality—MITI was famous for *not* hiring economists while CGP was recognized for its bias *for* hiring engineers.

As far as this study has been able to determine, none of the other studied agencies had an equivalent of DARPA's strict four-year term limit. MITI and Korea's Blue House Secretariat both held out the prospect of life-long job security, even if not in the agency itself (Johnson 1982; Kim 2011). MITI's class-based system and early retirements did, however, create rapid turnover at the top. Average tenure among MITI vice-ministers was just under two years, even shorter than the average two-and-a-half year tenures of DARPA directors prior to Tony Tether.[47]

Failure cases were sometimes equally small or smaller, also heterogeneous, and also selective in hiring. Kenya's Dream Team included fewer than ten people and Marcos' NEDA employed less than a hundred. Simply hiring "a hundred geniuses and a travel agent," using four-year contracts, and a reporting line to the prime minster seems unlikely to create the Internet or any other major transformations.

Programs, Approaches, and Decision-Making. It is in task management where one would expect to find the greatest differences between the examples of VC firms and DARPA, examined above, and most public agencies, even one as unusual as MITI. DARPA and VC firms have a certain virtue of simplicity: at root, they have a sum of money and must allocate it. As long as they retain their budget, they have autonomy in what they seek to do. Ministries, in contrast, set policies, regulate, frame legislation, and do much else. For many actions they may require cabinet or legislative action.

However, this distinction becomes blurred when one examines the details. As described above, autonomy is not inherent in VC firms and certainly not in DARPA. It is a product of their structural and both formal and informal features. It could be argued that, given the respective balance of executive and legislative branches in Japan and the United States, it is simpler for an agency to have a law passed in the former than to maintain a stable, autonomous budget in the latter (Wilson 1989).

Legal instruments through which MITI worked were often deliberately general and vague, with laws frequently amounting to only a dozen pages for a specific industry (Johnson 1982). Exogenous shocks, such as social turmoil or capital-account liberalization, interacting with fierce inter- and intra-ministerial policy battles, would result in new missions and alter the overall organizational thrust. Examples include income doubling through heavy industry and chemical industrialization and driving international competitiveness in high-value durable consumer goods.

These policy shifts were translated into enabling umbrella laws which, after further policy battles, became vague industry-specific laws. Once industry-specific laws were in place, detailed specific policies and actions were undertaken, often under younger officials willing to propose new ideas.

Given the national scale of the stakes, this process was naturally more complex, difficult, and political than the cascade from mission to approval in DARPA, let alone the decision-making processes of VC firms. Some features, however, were consistent in all three settings—particularly the combination of very high thresholds for the approval of strategic thrusts and programs and the considerable discretion allowed thereafter.

A similar pattern was observed in Korea, whose laws were often copied verbatim from their Japanese equivalents. In 1973, in combination with intense political turmoil, a heavy-industry and chemical-industrialization drive was launched in Korea, with automotive and steel among the priority sectors. Both "contradicted South Korea's national capabilities," given that "the South Korean auto industry was a graveyard of would-be *chaebol*" (Lee 2011) and that Korean steel mills offered "the world's worst business case" (Chang 2010). Both industries, though, had been in development for a decade and had umbrella laws creating space within which *chaebol* programs and packages of financing and equipment were pieced together by the Blue House Secretariat in coordination with the EPB and the Ministry of Commerce and Industry (Rhyu and Lew 2011; Lee 2011).

Failing to develop these industries was unacceptable—but policy approaches could be and were developed and discarded. It was only in the early- to late-1970s that developed policies bore fruit with the start of operations at POSCO (formerly Pohang Iron and Steel Company) in 1972 and the development of the Hyundai Pony in 1979. Both have had somewhat more distinguished lives than the many steel mills and national automotive companies with less troubled births.

Vested Interests and System Management. Given the difficulty of gaining access to tacit knowledge, it is not easy to determine the informal culture and processes within navigating agencies. Some tentative conclusions, however, may be drawn from existing literature and comparisons with the cases explored above.

This subsection focuses on difficult realities facing all such agencies—dealing with vested interests, coordinating with other agencies, and avoiding capture.

In dealing with vested interests the task of MITI and similar agencies becomes most overtly political. This is clearly not a problem faced by VC firms. Vested interests have been, at times, an issue for DARPA (particularly when DARPA has sought to fund technologies likely to disrupt incumbent industries) and remain a core problem facing ARPA-E (Bonvillian and Van Atta 2011). When faced with conflicts with vested interests, on multiple occasions DARPA, MITI, and others have not only used but effectively reshaped their surrounding networks, over a sustained period of time, to indirectly overcome or co-opt such interests—in preference to any direct confrontation.

The most striking success for MITI, in stark contrast to its failure to overcome the vested interests of the telecommunications industries, was its management of Japan's 1960s exit from coal mining—an industry fully as entrenched and politically powerful as telecommunications. In addressing Japanese coal mining MITI used its programs to develop low-cost, high-quality overseas supplies to detach Japanese coal-using industries from domestic coal supplies. At the same time MITI helped Japanese coal producers acquire mines abroad; launched retraining and other programs to gain the support of employees and local communities; and brought in influential academic and civil-society voices to assert the necessity for the nation to end domestic coal production.

Piece by piece, MITI detached members of the opposing coalition and lowered the costs of a transition away from domestic coal. Compared not only to MITI's later telecommunications experience, but also to the British exit from domestic coal production, the results were striking—even if the conflict left lasting scars within MITI.[48]

Generally MITI, CGP, and—perhaps most surprisingly—the Blue House Secretariat tended to avoid top-down control even when they possessed the ability to wield such authority. MITI, in fact, rarely even had such authority vis-à-vis its networks, with the private sector frequently rejecting its plans and contesting its policies. In response MITI focused on continuously forming and mobilizing external coalitions (Jansen 2009).

Faced with similar issues, Jean Monnet in France was able to ensure that the CGP had direct access to the prime minister, giving it implicit authority, but he had it work largely by suasion, influence, and the ability to bring information to the surface and share significant data. This did not mean that CGP did not attack vested interests—it did, and caused controversy by doing so—but CGP picked its battles shrewdly, prepared the ground carefully, and exhausted other options before making aggressive moves (Monnet 1978; Cazes and Mioche 1990).

Perhaps most surprisingly, given common perception, Park's Blue House Secretariat was careful in its use of authority. Park knew that "relying too much on staff from the Blue House Secretariat would demoralize the line ministries and make his coordination efforts harder" (Kim 2011).

It is important, though, not to underplay the importance of the resources these agencies could command. Their stock of financial and/or political capital was indispensable to getting the right people to attend the right meetings. But this capital was used implicitly more than explicitly. Doors were kept open by providing high-quality technical problem-solving and information—about other stakeholders, foreign markets, and high-level politics.

In contrast, Kenya's "Dream Team" was inserted into command-and-control relationships with Kenyan line ministries through being appointed secretaries or given seats on the boards of state-owned companies. The team seems to have concentrated little on building supporting coalitions and/or on information-gathering. Instead they created action plans and tried to command agendas through these plans. From the beginning they sought to attack vested interests, expecting that "political will" would carry through their agendas. The result was a rapid backlash quickly overwhelming the team's action plans.

Collusion, Capture, and Exit. As with DARPA and star scientists or research laboratories, MITI and similar agencies operated close to the boundary of collusion and regulatory capture with and by their countries' leading industrial firms. Most of these agencies were willing to appear captured by the best, as long as these firms remained at the apex of their nations' economies and did not decay in capabilities. Indeed many have considered this practice crucial to their success (Evans 1995).

As with DARPA, and indeed as with venture capital firms, the clarity and importance of the mission, and the consequences of not meeting it, were again crucial to maintaining the border between effectiveness and capture.

During the 1950s and 1960s this seemed, for example, to have been the case with MITI: as much as MITI appeared to have been captured by former state-owned steel firms—or in thrall to the textile industry—it continued to inflict short-term economic losses to both industries as long as these short-term economic losses benefitted the long-term goal of "catching up."[49]

> *For each given sector, one* **chaebol** *would be given a head start—but always with the knowledge that a competitor would soon be introduced*

Even if an agency is not intentionally collusive, unfortunately, there are well-recognized risks of unintentional capture by the firms in which capital and capabilities are concentrated. Such firms may then degenerate into "lazy monopolists." It is not at all clear that MITI avoided this, particularly in its later decades.

There is quite detailed information, though, regarding how a different agency managed to balance discipline and favoritism—at least for a while. That is Park Chung-Hee and the Blue House Secretariat's management of Korea's *chaebol*.

The secretariat's strategy was simple but effective: For each given sector, one *chaebol* would be given a head start—but always with the knowledge that a competitor would soon be introduced (whether in six months, one year, or two years was not specified). This planned introduction of a competitor was irrespective of the first *chaebol*'s performance, motivating it to create as large an initial lead as possible. Other *chaebols* would then vie to be the one supported as the designated competitor, often doing initial fact-finding work. This implicit threat of vigorous competition was even held over POSCO, the state-owned steel company, at least in its initial years (Rhyu and Lew 2011).

This strategy meant that the *chaebol* in a sector had to fear not the entry of small and medium enterprises, which they could probably easily defeat, but highly resourced, highly capable competitors of their own scale and ambition. This is similar to DARPA's creation of competitors to any existing concentration of capabilities, not randomly or from a "level playing field," but by inducing the entry of equally capable laboratories or spin-offs.[50]

This may suggest, perhaps simplistically, a "duopoly" rule: For any program necessarily drawing on a limited set of highly advanced capabilities, navigating agencies, by supporting the entry of credible competitors, should ensure that periods when a single entrant has monopolized a capability or industry are short. More generally, it may suggest this rule as a means for testing and measuring navigating agencies: Do they actively work to expand the set of firms with sufficient capabilities or, at the least, work to prevent the set of firms with sufficient capabilities from shrinking or stagnating for too long a time?

Most of these examples raise the question of when and how navigating agencies decided that an industry or a firm had crossed from cooperation to capture or from struggling to grow to failed attempt and, hence, when to exit an industry or persevere.

While more primary research, with access to archival materials, will be needed to reach firm conclusions, the examples of coal and textiles in Japan point in similar directions: when multiple approaches have been tried to "fix" an industry, including a concerted effort to form new capabilities, and not worked; when no new information could come to light on what to try next; when continued maintenance of the industry would jeopardize the mission; and when, as a result, a developmental coalition opposed to its maintenance is readily at hand; then it is time to exit.

Conclusions

A pattern of similarities in how some classic "navigating agencies" have implemented flexibly is summarized in Table 3. What might this mean for political leaders and policymakers, in Asia and elsewhere, struggling with problems that have no ready solution or seeking to reform agencies that have failed to be effective and flexible?

This question seems pertinent across Asia—with economies having gone through transformation but now competing on demanding technological frontiers; with others seeking to escape the "middle-income trap" by building innovative economies that are home to world-class competitors; and with still others seeking take-off and needing to upgrade industrial structures in the face of rapidly changing global value chains.

Asia has been home to a number of navigating agencies, some famous successes, some failures, and some both at different times.[51] The region's old path to prosperity and its current locus of competitiveness—high-volume manufacturing—is threatened with intense disruption from innovation-centered competition in the present and additive manufacturing and other new technologies in the future.

Table 3 below offers pragmatic possible strategies, organized, for consistency, following the analytical structure of this study. As indicated in the latter sections of this study, common threads run through these features and techniques. These common threads offer the basis, albeit as still-tentative theory, for a simpler, if higher-level, set of three strategies for flexibility:

1. *Macro discipline to micro autonomy*—A clear goal mattering to the survival of the political elite must cascade through "visionary" programs to multiple approaches via an approval process making program approval difficult but granting high operational autonomy thereafter.

2. *Acting through a (shaped) system*—The agency must be embedded in and implement these goals through surrounding systems. Nodes of these surrounding systems must be extended, combined, and induced by the navigating agency to create the *capabilities* and *coalitions* needed for success—with these actions enabled through the promise of access to incremental resources.

3. *Information overload*—Processes must emphasize information transmittal, using formal meetings and processes as a skeleton with the flesh provided by frequent informal contacts. Accountability and concern must be less for the failure of an approach than for not knowing or understanding the causes for the failure or for not being able to extract useful information from the failure.

In sum, flexible implementation is indirect; has information as its lifeblood; and mediates extreme high-level discipline to extreme ground-level autonomy via long-range programs.

These strategies remain theory, untested on cases outside of those from which they are derived, and therefore prompting further research. If validated, though, these strategies have a number of clear implications.

First, each of the features noted in Table 3, and described in the narrative, may be traced to one or a combination of these strategies (Figure 1). These strategies, working together, can likewise account for overcoming the problems of flexibility described in the introduction. Use of a high approval-threshold for programs and a low approval-threshold for approaches, for example, concentrates risk in the lower-level tasks. There it is distributed throughout the system, reducing exit costs for the agency. Macro-discipline governs discretion, which then takes action through combining nodes within the system while continually generating large amounts of information. The availability of this thick information flow allows recombination of nodes on the fly, reducing uncertainty and the chances of having to exit.

Second, these strategies may also account for the controversy surrounding attribution for several of the cases above: an agency pursuing long-term, macro goals through indirect, micro actions will—even if it is effective—leave few-to-no traces detectable through statistical tests.

Third, the strategies are interdependent. One cannot manage a complex system without information and autonomy. The political costs of granting autonomy to an agency supplied with adequate resources and authority to act directly would likely be insurmountable—no matter the amount of "political will" available.[52]

Indeed, the obsession with "political will" in much of current policy discourse seems, in light of these strategies, misplaced. Equally so does the vogue for "private sector" solutions—whether considering

Table 3. Fourteen Techniques for Flexible Implementation

Structural Characteristics

1   *Threats made politically salient to a broad section of the political elite*

2   *Clear and simple missions* whose achievement will answer these threats and whose failure will make their realization more likely

3   *Ambition and simplicity of measurement* in defining goals, more so than attribution (removing the ability to "fudge" success is more important than being able to attribute it)

4   *Strong but delayed incentives* both collective (the end of the agency if it fails overall) and individual (career-making or career-breaking)

5   *Surrounding systems of diverse capabilities,* whether to identify solutions (e.g., diversity of firms and research institutes) or to implement them (e.g., civilian customers and/or military services)

Formal and Informal Techniques

1   *Build developmental coalitions rather than relying on (or waiting for) political will;* bring together previously unconnected capabilities, using political capital as the incentive, rather than expending political capital in command-and-control and close monitoring.

2   *Distinguish between "programs" and "approaches."* Programs address high-level outcomes (e.g., develop an automotive industry) while approaches involve policies and investments which may or may not advance that outcome (e.g., add a manager to a start-up team, subsidize Hyundai).

3   *Bias programs towards consensus and caution* to limit broad failures. *Bias approaches towards autonomy* to limit missed opportunities. Use the Heilmeier Catechism or similar tools for decisions at both levels.

4   *Keep the agency small.* Do not grow past roughly a hundred staff and, if possible, stay smaller. Maintain a hiring bias toward operational experience (bureaucratic or industrial) over theory—although not dogmatically.

5   *Over-invest in obtaining, sharing, and using information,* formal and informal: utilize frequent (weekly) meetings focused on problems not process and "observer rights" or the equivalent.

6   *Use quantitative goals as a tool in people management rather than as a substitute for people management.* Use simple, clear, but difficult goals to orient action, bring information to the surface, trigger problem-solving, and adjust opinions—primarily regarding people and capabilities (*who* more than *what*).

7   *When faced with a potential failure:* a) bring more information to the surface; b) add new capabilities; c) adjust the team or coalition; or d) find a new, equally ambitious, goal. Only after these approaches have been tried should exit be considered. Use such tools as the questions: *Can it still be a home run? If yes, what can we fix? Who can we add to improve the team?*

Table 3. Fourteen Techniques for Flexible Implementation (continued)	
8	*Keep quiet at first.* Building a record of success can cushion the political costs of exit before exposing the agency to attack.
9	*Generate additional entries to prevent the risk of capture.* Support the entry of credible competitors to ensure that periods when a capability or industry is monopolized by a single entrant are short.

annual bonuses, exclusively private-sector hiring, or charismatic lead-ers. If anything, VC firms resemble DARPA—and, one could even argue, MITI—more than they resemble larger "private equity" firms. Still, these noted strategies clearly require *some* amount of political capital, even if it might rarely need to be spent, and they require more-than-normal leeway vis-à-vis "typical" public-sector processes.

These three strategies suggest three core tasks for political lead-ers and policymakers seeking to create or reform navigating agen-cies to deal with Asia's uncertain policy challenges:

> *The obsession with 'political will'—and the vogue for 'private sector' solutions—in current policy discourse seems, in light of these strategies, misplaced*

1. Define a singular long-range goal, easy to measure and whose fail-ure threatens the survival of the political elite, and link a tiered-approval process, as described above, to responses to this goal.
2. Define the system in which the navigating agency will be embed-ded and obtain for the navigating agency the financial and/or po-litical resources needed to allow it both autonomy and the ability to induce action within its surrounding system as well as to shape that system over the medium- to long-term.[53]
3. Establish management processes and hiring rules generating thick information flows and make managing these thick information flows the agency's day-to-day (versus long-range) accountability.

Just as VC firms with early successes can later take greater risks and sustain more failure, navigating agencies successful in their first ini-

Figure 1. Three Strategies Aggregating Techniques for Flexible Implementation

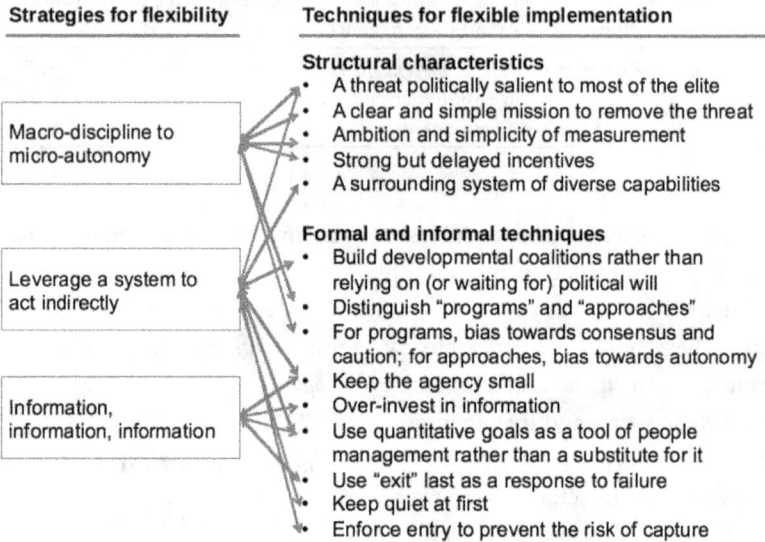

Strategies for flexibility	Techniques for flexible implementation
	Structural characteristics • A threat politically salient to most of the elite • A clear and simple mission to remove the threat • Ambition and simplicity of measurement • Strong but delayed incentives • A surrounding system of diverse capabilities
Macro-discipline to micro-autonomy	
Leverage a system to act indirectly	**Formal and informal techniques** • Build developmental coalitions rather than relying on (or waiting for) political will • Distinguish "programs" and "approaches" • For programs, bias towards consensus and caution; for approaches, bias towards autonomy • Keep the agency small • Over-invest in information • Use quantitative goals as a tool of people management rather than a substitute for it • Use "exit" last as a response to failure • Keep quiet at first • Enforce entry to prevent the risk of capture
Information, information, information	

tiatives accrue political capital making securing cooperation and handling expected later failures easier. Navigating agencies should thus avoid acquiring too public a profile too soon as that may make them more vulnerable and invite attacks before these agencies are capable of responding to such attacks.[54]

Diagnostic questions useful in attempting to reform such agencies might include:

1. Is the mission clear, simple, long-term, and unambiguous? In translating that mission into programs, does the agency set a high threshold for approval? Conversely, once programs are approved, do the programs have the resources and scope to act autonomously? Do programs successfully address the Heilmeier Catechism?

2. Is the agency embedded in a system? Does it seek to bypass, overcome, control, or overwhelm that system? Conversely, is it ignored by that system? When was the last time the agency facilitated the creation of a new node in the system? When was the last time the agency generated a credible new entrant to compete with an

incumbent within that system? In the agency's programs, what is the ratio between its funds and those of others (or, how much does it leverage the resources of others when it acts?)? Does the agency build developmental coalitions or complain about an absence of political will?

3. Does the agency generate thick information flows? Is there more accountability for program failure or for not knowing the causes of the failure? What is its internal and external meeting cycle? Can key staff, from memory, describe the capabilities of all agency partners? What percentage of these partners are contacted weekly? Can agency staff describe each other's portfolios, including instances of failure and of rescued near-failures?

And there must be the question of scope of application: When is such an agency desirable or even possible? As described in the introduction, there are issues of discipline, or even of simple coordination, where other institutional forms might be more appropriate. Such issues, however, may involve coordination and learning and thus offer synergies with the second and third strategies. There is also the question of size: an agency of at most a hundred staff may be limited in the size of the system it can affect—though Japan's history indicates any such threshold may be quite high.[55]

Most pertinent, though, is the difficulty of the first strategy— goal-setting. There can and will be instances where there simply is no credible threat to the survival of the political elites or basis for consensus among the political elites. Low levels of active participation or a fractured society provide little basis for an overwhelming consensus and/or few channels to translate any possible consensus into political pressure. Aid-soaked and heterogeneous states may be particularly infertile ground for such agencies.

A context of political leaders, including those in electoral democracies, declaiming about "jobs" is also not enough.[56] This is not to make any general statement about electoral democracies: Japan, even if dominated by a single party, shows otherwise—as, of course, does DARPA in the United States. It is only to say that substantial rhetorical and political effort must go into the framing of threats and missions before the full range of capabilities described here may be employed to their full effect.[57]

The problem of flexible implementation and, arguably, that of structural transformation itself, then becomes one of rhetoric and politics. Given the complexity of problems confronting political leaders and policymakers over the next decade, in Asia and elsewhere, few problems could be more important.

Endnotes

1. This paragraph draws on a wide literature on dynamic resource allocation, productivity growth, and structural transformation, among which Khan (2009) and Bartelsman, Haltiwanger, and Scarpetta (2011) provide useful summaries. It also draws on a wide literature about the policy effects and problems of industrial growth, among which the following could be highlighted: Hirschman (1958); Gelb, Meyer, and Ramachandran (2014); Killick (1978); Lin (2012); and Robinson (2009) and Pritchett, Woolcock, and Andrews (2012).

2. This is neither a binary nor an objective distinction. Various observers might see the same problem, and its proposed solution, differently. Technocratic officials and development agencies tend to see problems as being "solved" after the policy-analysis phase is completed whereas politicians, institutional insiders, and scholars of the "new public sector reform" (Blum, Manning, and Srivastava 2012) and "new industrial policy" (Rodrik 2004) tend to see a problem as unsolved if the solution is not workable within institutional and political constraints.

3. This assertion may seem controversial, given the EPB's canonical role in South Korea's development. However, detailed studies of the EPB reveal that, in most instances, it believed it had the "right" answer and so it was solving discipline and coordination problems. The Blue House Secretariat, by contrast, was less certain, more adaptable and, in balancing between ministries, more flexible.

4. This list derives from the literature on agency management, stretching back to Wilson (1989), as well as conversations with Charles Sabel and our colleagues Thomas Kenyon and Joanna Watkins.

5. It is reportedly not possible to test even simple formal hypotheses about management structure and long-run performance. Personal communication with Andrew Metrick, professor of finance and management, Yale University.

6. In the VC industry, "exit" usually refers to liquidating an equity position, whether through sale of the equity or distribution of shares post-IPO. To maintain

continuity with the rest of this study, here "exit" will be used to denote withdrawal from a potentially failing investment.

7. Some firms also have a role called "partner," described as being a candidate general partner, with many of the same responsibilities but without ownership in the firm. One GP described it as akin to being an "associate professor," by contrast to having tenure.

8. Waldeck, Wainwright, and Blaydon (2003). Empirically, Hall and Woodward (2010) examined roughly 22,000 venture-backed companies, finding that a third were closed or worth nothing, forty percent were still active, and roughly a quarter had been acquired.

9. Interviews with current and former general partners, as well as with academics specializing in this field, are the basis of these observations. Future stages of this research could include interviews with investees. Thus the following impressions about how "typical" VC firms might operate largely reflect the views from within VC firms.

10. Personal communication with general partner (names of GPs withheld to protect confidentiality).

11. This may, of course, change if the recent spectacular valuation of Tesla is repeated for other clean-technology companies.

12. What this means can best be illustrated by the varying fortunes of Silicon Valley, Boston, and the greater Washington, DC, area: They have relatively similar business environments and they all host a similar concentration of world-class research institutions yet there is a vast gulf between them, judging by the size and outcomes of their VC industries. It is difficult to specify precisely the causes for this divergence but what literature there is, echoed in interviews, suggests that the principal differences are the local supply of entrepreneurial talent and the propensity toward openness and collaboration among the institutes and firms in the area (Saxenian 1996). The ultimate causes of those differences are not entirely clear but one potential cause is the larger role played by the US Department of Defense in IT and Silicon Valley in its early years when the DoD had a strong commitment to open information sharing among its recipients. See, for example, Ruttan (2006) and the discussion of DARPA below. On the other hand, Massachusetts is not deficient in its ties to the defense industry.

13. Personal communication with Andrew Metrick, professor of finance and management, Yale University.

14. Personal communication with a GP.

15. Personal communication with a GP. As noted above, however, sufficient data does not exist to determine the strength of this pattern.

16. Personal communication with Andrew Metrick and with John Boyle, director of engagement, Purdue West Coast Partnership Center.

17. The following is a composite picture drawn from all our interviews, in which this topic was of core interest.

18. It is notable, in this light, that it is difficult to find successful VC firms with a captive investor, such as a family wealth fund. The only exceptions to this feature seems to be the very best funds, such as Kleiner Perkins or Sequoia, whose track records might remove fears of a lack of funding. However, such funds seem to have such a strongly ingrained culture that they compensate for the lower level of threat. In addition, they have the path-dependent advantages of success described here.

19. Across multiple decades, DARPA has played a symbiotic role with the VC industry in creating the IT revolution. See, among many others, Fong (2001) and Mazzucato (2013) for the outsider view, and Janeway (2012) for the insider agreement. Former DARPA officials point out that almost every component of the iPhone traces its origin to the agency.

20. Observers note that, though DARPA reports formally to the Assistant Secretary of Defense for Research and Engineering (ASDR&E), informally it has managed to remove itself from this reporting line.

21. Adaptive Execution Office (AEO), Defense Sciences Office (DSO), Information Innovation Office (I20), Microsystems Technology Office (MTO), Strategic Technology Office (STO), and Tactical Technology Office (TTO).

22. Personal communication with Robert F. Leheny, formerly program manager, office director and deputy director, DARPA, currently senior research staff, Institute for Defense Analyses. See also Carleton (2010) and Fuchs (2010) for an elaboration of the approval process, both in recent years and as it has changed over the decades.

23. A few examples of stand-alone studies include Fong (2000), which places DARPA within the changing patterns of US industrial policy; Carleton (2010), which examines in depth the technology-visioning process within DARPA; Fuchs (2010), which considers informal processes of idea generation; and Piore (2011), which considers flexibility in depth, also as related to informal processes, and situated in the public-sector-management literature—and to which this paper owes a substantial debt.

24. Indeed, most of these customers or implementers "cherry pick" DARPA's most promising ideas, something particularly true of venture capital firms, so that DARPA has come to be, in some ways, a market-maker in radical innovation through its ability to provide credible signals. The authors are grateful to Richard Van Atta for this observation.

25. Personal communication with Michael Piore, professor of economics, Massachusetts Institute of Technology.

26. This is not only the case in bureaucracies, but in venture capital as well. One of our GP interviewees mentioned that a number of VC funds have run into trouble in the last decade precisely because they did not provide long-term internal careers for their most promising young general partners.

27. For example, Tony Tether is known to have imposed such a test very strictly, in large part as he did think the agency had lost discipline. George Heilmeier (director of DARPA, 1975-1976) also imposed it often, to the point of not approving the stealth fighter program until the air force had agreed to be a client. Personal communication with Richard Van Atta.

28. Named after George Heilmeier. Original version: http://cseweb.ucsd.edu/~ddahlstr/misc/heilmeier.html .

29. The practice is uncommon enough that there was some contention among interviewees about whether it even takes place—but was attested to by former PMs as occurring on occasion.

30. Personal communication with Michael Piore.

31. Personal Communication with Robert Leheny and Marko Slusarczuk. For the industry-structure argument, see Fuchs (2010).

32. We are grateful to Richard Van Atta for this phrasing.

33. Personal communication with Michael Piore.

34. Personal communication with Richard Van Atta.

35. Ibid.

36. The National Science Foundation, for example, has a budget of $7 billion, for a vastly wider mandate. DARPA's $3 billion annual appropriation is one of the largest research budgets in the federal government.

37. Mick, J. 2011. "DARPA Auditors Probe Nepotism, Corruption Allegations." *DailyTech,* August 17.

38. Personal communication with Michael Piore.

39. We are grateful to one of our reviewers for this insight.

40. Personal communication with Richard Van Atta.

41. Personal communication with Marko Slusarczuk.

42. The classic account in Johnson (1982) still serves as well as any other in this regard. A particularly vivid example is Sahashi Shigeru's clash with Maruzen Oil Company, when personal losses were inflicted on a private sector representative

—to the substantial political cost of MITI itself—in the name of national catching up (see pp. 260-61).

43. This goal might be contrasted with the announced goals of contemporaneous authoritarians in Latin America—such as the regimes in Brazil, Mexico, and Chile—with their oft-repeated, vague goals incorporating "patriotism, modernization, public order, morality, anticommunism, measures against corruption, economic reorganization and growth" (Dominguez 2011).

44. "Dream Team was All About Suing for Peace with Donors." 2012. *Daily Nation,* November 28. http://www.nation.co.ke/News/politics/Dream-Team-was-all-about-suing-for-peace/-/1064/1632488/-/qbgkgz/-/index.html .

45. This is not to say that these goals are not worthwhile, merely that if, lacking the courage of prioritization, they are pursued simultaneously and with the same priority as growth, the result is a mission that is ill-conducive to the kind of agency under investigation.

46. Personal communications with MITI officials. This is corroborated by a count of the positions at section chief and above in the organization charts presented in Johnson (1982).

47. Compare Johnson (1982), Annex A, with Fuchs (2010), Table 1.

48. Personal communications with MITI officials. Young officials in MITI today speak of this story as one "that could be told by everyone in the Ministry, but no one really likes talking about it." This deepens the contrast to the British experience exiting the coal industry in the 1980s. In one case, political will was abundant; in the other, it was almost unimportant. In one case, it left scars on the public; in the other, it left scars on those who accomplished it.

49. The example of Sahashi is again germane. Likewise, although Ike (1980) illustrates the domestic measures taken to buttress the Japanese textile industry, these seem relatively minor compared to the protectionism often associated with this industry, and—as Chibber (2006) shows—at the same time Japan was actively developing the South Korean industry, given its far lower labor costs and ability to absorb Japanese capital goods. Machinery mattered for "catching up" far more than textiles did and so received priority.

50. It is also reminiscent, in some ways, of an earlier Japanese story of Mitsubishi in the late nineteenth century. At the point where it was in danger of becoming a "lazy monopolist," a change in political factions led to the introduction of a highly capitalized, state-sponsored competitor. While Mitsubishi won the ensuing competition, it became vastly more efficient and its prices fell by a large amount (Yamamura 1967). It is likewise reminiscent of the old US military policy of "dual sourcing," which was jettisoned in the 1990s, after analyses indicated it increased the prices of individual procurements, without considering the effect on long-term competition in the defense industry and, hence, the pricing power and capabilities of defense firms (Ruttan 2006).

51. Where, in addition, many attempts have faltered to build DARPA-like structures and VC industries. A number of our interviewees reported being repeatedly invited to East Asia to give seminars and talks on the DARPA model.

52. The hierarchical control that would have to be vested in such an agency would create counter-reactions, exclusion, and tacit hiding, which even autocratic leaders would find difficult to countermand. Even Park Chung-Hee, the embodiment of political will for development, worried about the effect of demoralizing line ministries. More extreme, even Stalin in 1948 lacked full control over his bureaucracy (Belova and Lazarev 2013), and he hardly lacked political will.

53. For example, giving to MITI the resources of a DARPA—flexible budget and autonomous hiring rules—would be unlikely to help it induce change, given the structure of Japan's bureaucracy. Conversely, attempting to give DARPA the power of a MITI would be likely only to overwhelm its autonomy and hence its effectiveness.

54. This might be named the "ARPA-E conundrum," given how acutely the problem faces this agency. The authors are grateful to Richard Van Atta for this observation.

55. On the other hand, it is noticeable that China has not had a nodal agency of this type, at least centrally, but has rather harnessed its decentralized structure to enable flexibility (Heilmann 2008; Xu 2011). It might, though, be possible for the model to work better within a sub-unit (e.g., a sector or province) of a larger country and the leading group for economic reform, announced at the Third Plenum in October 2013, may, depending on its form, provide an interesting test case.

56. Elections provide some, albeit weak, incentives for growth to politicians who might serve as clients. The "economic hypothesis of accountability" has some empirical support—but mostly for large shocks, not "business as usual" (Kriesi 2013). This is particularly the case where alternate electoral strategies are available, such as those based on identity or issue (Chhibber and Nooruddin 2004), or the cohesion of a party machine which requires rent distribution and patronage. Coalition governments with parties mobilizing identity or social-issue blocs may then also be particularly infertile ground for such agencies and teams.

57. For example, the inverse of "rich country, strong army" is "poor country, weak army"; it is not clear what the inverse of a "new society" is or why a member of the political elite would be threatened by it. Moreover, just because a speaker thinks the political elite should care about a threat does not mean they will; lengthy disquisitions on the perils of social injustice or environmental degradation are unlikely to be sufficient.

Bibliography

Avnimelech, G., M. Kenney, and M. Teubal. 2003. "Building Venture Capital Industries: Understanding the U.S. and Israeli Experiences." *BRIE Working Paper* 160. Berkeley Roundtable on the International Economy, University of California at Berkeley and the Graduate School of International Relations and Pacific Studies, University of California at San Diego.

Bartelsman, E., J. Haltiwanger, and S. Scarpetta. 2011. "Cross Country Differences in Productivity: The Role of Allocative Efficiency," mimeo.

Belova, E., and V. Lazarev. 2013. *Funding Loyalty: The Economics of the Communist Party.* New Haven, CT: Yale University Press.

Bennis, W.G., and P.W. Biederman. 1997. *Organizing Genius.* New York: Basic Books.

Berger, S., with the MIT Task Force on Production in the Innovation Economy. 2013. Making in America: From Innovation to Market. Cambridge, MA: The MIT Press.

Bernanke, B.S. 2013. "The Ten Suggestions." Remarks at Baccalaureate Ceremony, Princeton University, Princeton, NJ.

Blum, J., N. Manning, and V. Srivastava. 2012. "Public Sector Management Reform: Toward a Problem-Solving Approach." *Economic Premise* 100. Washington, DC: The World Bank.

Bonvillian, W. 2006. "Power Play: The DARPA Model and U.S. Energy Policy." *The American Interest* ii (2, November/December). http://tppserver.mit.edu/esd801/pdfs/WBB.pdf .

Bonvillian, W.B., and R. Van Atta. 2011. "ARPA-E and DARPA: Applying the DARPA Model to Energy Innovation." *The Journal of Technology Transfer* 36 (5): 469–513.

Carleton, T.L. 2010. "The Value of Vision in Radical Technological Innovation," PhD diss., Stanford University Department of Mechanical Engineering.

Cazes, B. 1990. "Indicative Planning in France." *Journal of Comparative Economics* 14 (4): 607–20.

Cazes, B., and P. Mioche. 1990. *Modernisation ou Décadence: Études, Témoignages et Documents sur la Planification Française.* Aix-en-Provence, France: Université de Provence Service des Publications.

Chang, H.J. 2010. *23 Things They Don't Tell You About Capitalism.* New York: Bloomsbury Publishing.

Chhibber, P., and I. Nooruddin. 2004. "Do Party Systems Count? The Number of Parties and Government Performance in the Indian States." *Comparative Political Studies,* 37 (2), 152–187.

Chibber, V. 2006. *Locked in Place: State-Building and Late Industrialization in India.* Princeton, NJ: Princeton University Press.

Choi, B.S. 1987. "The Structure of the Economic Policy-Making Institutions in Korea and the Strategic Role of the Economic Planning Board." *Korean Journal of Policy Studies,* vol.2, pp. 1–25.

Ciccantell, P. and S. Bunker. 2002. "International Inequality in the Age of Globalization: Japanese Economic Ascent and the Restructuring of the Capitalist World-Economy." *Journal of World-Systems Research* viii (1, winter): 62–98.

Corbett, J.S. 1911. *Some Principles of Maritime Strategy.* London: Longmans, Green, and Co.

Crawcour, E.S. 1989. "Industrialization and Technological Change, 1885–1920." *The Cambridge History of Japan,* vol. 6, ch. 8, 383–450.

Criscuolo, A., and V. Palmade. 2008. "Reform Teams: How the Most Successful Reformers Organized Themselves." *Public Policy for the Private Sector* 318. Washington, DC: The World Bank.

Dominguez, J.I. 2011. "The Perfect Dictatorship? South Korea versus Argentina, Brazil, Chile, and Mexico." In *The Park Chung-Hee Era: The Transformation of South Korea,* ch. 20, edited by B-K Kim and E.F. Vogel. Cambridge, MA: Harvard University Press.

Dower, J.W. 2000. *Embracing Defeat: Japan in the Wake of World War II.* New York: WW Norton & Company.

Dugan, R. 2012. "From Mach-20 Glider to Humming Bird Drone." TED Talk. http://www.ted.com/talks/regina_dugan_from_mach_20_glider_to_humming_bird_drone.html .

Evans, P. 1995. *Embedded Autonomy*. Princeton, NJ: Princeton University Press.

Fong, G.R. 2000. "Breaking New Ground or Breaking the Rules: Strategic Reorientation in US Industrial Policy." *International Security* 25 (2): 152–86.

Fong, G.R. 2001. "ARPA Does Windows: The Defense Underpinning of the PC Revolution." *Business and Politics* 3 (3): 213–37.

Fuchs, E.R. 2010. "Rethinking the Role of the State in Technology Development: DARPA and the Case for Embedded Network Governance." *Research Policy* 39 (9): 1133–47.

Gelb, A., C.J. Meyer, and V. Ramachandran. 2014. "Development as Diffusion - Manufacturing Productivity and Sub-Saharan Africa's Missing Middle." CGD Working Paper 357. Washington, DC: Center for Global Development.

George, A.L. and A. Bennett. 2005. *Case Studies and Theory Development in the Social Sciences*. Cambridge, MA: The MIT Press.

Gibson, C.C., K. Andersson, E. Ostrom, and S. Shivakumar. 2005. *The Samaritan's Dilemma: The Political Economy of Development Aid*. New York: Oxford University Press.

Gilson, R.J., C.F. Sabel, and R.E. Scott. 2009. "Contracting for Innovation: Vertical Disintegration and Interfirm Collaboration." *Columbia Law Review* 431–502.

Hall, R.E., and S.E. Woodward. 2010. "The Burden of the Nondiversifiable Risk of Entrepreneurship." *American Economic Review* 100 (3): 1163–94.

Heilmann, S. 2008. "From Local Experiments to National Policy: The Origins of China's Distinctive Policy Process." *The China Journal* 59 (January): 1–30. http://www.jstor.org/stable/20066378 .

Heinemann, R.L. 1981. "Blue Eagle or Black Buzzard? The National Recovery Administration in Virginia." *The Virginia Magazine of History and Biography* 89 (1): 90–100.

Hirschman, A.O. (1958). *The Strategy of Economic Development*. New Haven: Yale University Press.

Hirschman, A.O. 1970. *Exit, Voice, and Loyalty: Responses to Decline in Firms, Organizations, and States*. Cambridge, MA: Harvard University Press.

Hutchcroft, P.D. 2011. "Dictatorship, Development, and Plunder: The Regimes of Park Chung-Hee and Ferdinand Marcos Compared." In *The Park Chung-Hee Era: The Transformation of South Korea*, ch. 19, edited by B-K Kim and E.F. Vogel. Cambridge, MA: Harvard University Press.

Hwang, V. 2012. "What's the Difference Between Private Equity and Venture Capital?," *Forbes,* October 1. http://www.forbes.com/sites/victorhwang/2012/10/01/presidential-debate-primer-whats-the-difference-between-private-equity-and-venture-capital/ .

Hwang, V., and G. Horowitt. 2012. *The Rainforest: The Secret to Building the Next Silicon Valley.* Los Altos Hills, CA: Regenwald.

Ike, B. 1980. "The Japanese Textile Industry: Structural Adjustment and Government Policy." *Asian Survey* 20 (5): 532–51.

Inspector General, United States Department of Defense. 2013. *Defense Advanced Research Projects Agency's Ethics Program Met Federal Government Standards.* Report No. DODIG-2013-03 (January 24). http://www.dodig.mil/PUBS/documents/DODIG-2013-039.pdf .

Janeway, W.H. 2012. *Doing Capitalism in the Innovation Economy: Markets, Speculation and the State.* Cambridge, UK: Cambridge University Press.

Jansen, M.B. 2009. *The Making of Modern Japan.* Cambridge, MA: Harvard University Press.

Johnson, C. 1982. *MITI and the Japanese Miracle: The Growth of Industrial Policy, 1925–1975.* Redwood City, CA: Stanford University Press.

Kaplan, S., and P. Strömberg. 2000a. "Financial Contracting Theory Meets the Real World: An Empirical Analysis of Venture Capital Contracts." *NBER Working Paper No. 7660.* National Bureau of Economic Research, Cambridge, MA. http://www.nber.org/papers/w7660 .

Kaplan, S., and P. Strömberg. 2000b. "How Do Venture Capitalists Choose Investments?" (unpublished manuscript, August 2000). http://www.hec.fr/var/corporate/storage/original/application/2bab283a1bb53fc01cf38f0629bb59c4.pdf .

Kaplan, S., P. Strömberg, and B. Sensoy. 2002. "How Well do Venture Capital Databases Reflect Actual Investments?" (unpublished manuscript, September). http://ssrn.com/abstract=939073

Killick, T. 1978. *Development Economics in Action: A Study of Economic Policies in Ghana.* London: Heinemann.

Khan, M. 2009. *Learning, Technology Acquisition and Governance Challenges in Developing Countries.* London: School of Oriental and African Studies.

Kim, B-K. 2011. "The Leviathan: Economic Bureaucracy under Park." In *The Park Chung-Hee Era: The Transformation of South Korea*, ch. 7, edited by B-K Kim and E.F. Vogel. Cambridge, MA: Harvard University Press.

Kim, B-K, and E.F. Vogel, eds. 2011. *The Park Chung-Hee Era: The Transformation of South Korea*. Cambridge, MA: Harvard University Press.

Kriesi, H. 2013. "The Political Consequences of the Great Recession in Europe: Electoral Punishment and Popular Protest." Public lecture at The London School of Economics and Political Science. http://www2.lse.ac.uk/publicEvents/events/2013/01/20130130t1830vHKT.aspx .

Lee, N-Y. 2011. "The Automobile Industry." In *The Park Chung-Hee Era: The Transformation of South Korea*, ch. 10, edited by B-K Kim and E.F. Vogel. Cambridge, MA: Harvard University Press.

Lin, J.Y. 2012. *New Structural Economics: A Framework For Rethinking Development and Policy*. Washington, DC: The World Bank.

Mazzucato, M. 2013. *The Entrepreneurial State: Debunking Public vs Private Sector Myths*. London: Anthem Press.

Monnet, J. 1978. *Memoirs*, 1st US edition. New York: Doubleday & Company.

Mothershed, A.A. "Perception Is Reality, or Is It? A Case Study of Four Department of Defense (DoD) Procurement Scandals. Does Media Coverage Lead to Procurement Reform?" LL.M thesis, The George Washington University Law School, 2011. Proquest (1505937)

Okazaki, T. 2001. "The Government-Firm Relationship in Postwar Japan: The Success and Failure of Bureau Pluralism." In *Rethinking the East Asian Miracle*, edited by J.E. Stiglitz and S. Yusuf, 323–43. New York: Oxford University Press.

Penenberg, A. 2011. "Siri-ously DARPA." *Fast Company*, October 5. http://www.fastcompany.com/1785221/siri-ously-darpa.

Piore, M. 2011. "Beyond Markets: Sociology, Street-level Bureaucracy, and the Management of the Public Sector." *Regulation & Governance* 5 (1, March): 145–64.

Posen, A. 2002. "Unchanging Innovation and Changing Economic Performance in Japan." *Institute for International Economics Working Paper* 01–05.

Pritchett, L., M. Woolcock, and M. Andrews. 2012. "Looking Like a State: Techniques of Persistent Failure in State Capability for Implementation." *CID Working Paper* 239 (June).

Rhyu, S-Y, and S-J Lew. 2011. "Pohang Iron & Steel Company." In *The Park Chung-Hee Era: The Transformation of South Korea*, ch. 11, edited by B-K Kim and E.F. Vogel. Cambridge, MA: Harvard University Press.

Robinson, J. 2009. *Industrial Policy and Development: A Political Economy Perspective.* Washington, DC: The World Bank.

Robles, S.G. 2011. "Building a Local Venture Capital Industry in Latin America and the Caribbean." *Latin American Law & Business Report*, June.

Rodrik, D. 2004. "Industrial Policy for the Twenty-First Century." *Center for Economic Policy Research,* CEPR Discussion Paper no. 4767.

Rodrik, D. 2008. "The New Development Economics: We Shall Experiment, but How Shall We Learn?" *HKS Working Paper* no. RWP08-055. HKS Faculty Research Working Papers Series.

Ruttan, V.W. 2006. *Is War Necessary for Economic Growth?: Military Procurement And Technology Development.* New York: Oxford University Press.

Sah, R.K., and J. Stiglitz. 1986. "The Architecture of Economic Systems: Hierarchies and Polyarchies." *American Economic Review* 76 (4, September): 716–27.

Sah, R.K., and J.E. Stiglitz. 1988. "Committees, Hierarchies and Polyarchies." *The Economic Journal* 98 (391): 451–70.

Sakakibara, M., and D.S. Cho. 2002. "Cooperative R&D in Japan and Korea: A Comparison of Industrial Policy." *Research Policy* 31 (5): 673–92.

Saxenian, A. 1996. *Regional Advantage: Culture and Competition in Silicon Valley and Route 128.* Cambridge, MA: Harvard University Press.

Skocpol, T., and K. Finnegold. 1982. "State Capacity and Economic Intervention in the Early New Deal." *Political Science Quarterly* 97 (2): 255–78.

Tett, G. 2013. "Markets Insight: Venture Capital Funding Misses Out on Bull Run." *Financial Times,* May 23.

Van Atta, R. 2013. "Emerging Technology and Security" (unpublished lecture notes).

Waldeck, A., F. Wainwright, and C. Blaydon. 2003. *Note on Venture Capital Portfolio Management.* Case # 5-0016. Dartmouth College Tuck School of Business. http://cpee.tuck.dartmouth.edu/uploads/documents/portfolio_management.pdf .

Watkins, J., W. Dorotinsky, N. Manning, J. Brumby, and T. Thomas. 2010. *GET Note: Center of Government Delivery Units.* Washington, DC: World Bank.

Weber, M. 1978. *Economy and Society*, 2 vols., edited by G. Roth and C. Wittich [original German edition 1956]. Berkeley, CA: University of California Press.

Wilson, J.Q. 1989. *Bureaucracy: What Government Agencies Do And Why They Do It*. New York: Basic Books.

Xu, C. 2011. "The Fundamental Institutions of China's Reforms and Development." *Journal of Economic Literature* 49 (4): 1076–1151.

Yamamura, K. 1967. "The Founding of Mitsubishi: A Case Study in Japanese Business History." *The Business History Review* 141–60.

Acknowledgments

The authors wish to pay special thanks to Thomas Kenyon (The World Bank) and Richard Van Atta (the Institute for Defense Analyses) for their generous time commitments and extensive inputs to this paper. For comments which substantially improved this paper, we would also like to thank Dieter Ernst (East-West Center); our commenters during The World Bank's internal review, Michael Piore (MIT) and William Dorotinsky, Joanna Watkins, and Vincent Palmade (The World Bank); and our anonymous reviewers. In drafting this paper, we received invaluable guidance from Charles Sabel (Columbia Law School) as well as from Ivan Rossignol, Stefano Negri, sand Austin Kilroy at The World Bank. Carey Treado (University of Pittsburgh) provided us both literature references and invaluable perspectives on startups seeking venture capital funding and on exploring DARPA programs. Christopher Colford, also at The World Bank, provided invaluable editorial support. We are very grateful to Andrew Metrick, professor of finance and management, Yale University; John Boyle, director of engagement, Purdue West Coast Partnership Center; Ashmeet Sidana, general partner, Foundation Capital; Jim Barrett, general partner, New Enterprise Associates; and Alfred Lin, partner, Sequoia Capital, for fruitful discussions on venture capital. We are also very grateful to Robert F. Leheny, Marko Slusarczuk, and Josh Alspector of the Institute for Defense Analyses for fruitful discussions on DARPA. Special thanks go to Paul Holland, general partner, Foundation Capital, for his strong and continued cooperation and support. We are likewise very grateful to the current and former

MITI and METI officials who gave us their time and to Shiori Oni-shi of The World Bank who facilitated those consultations. We are grateful to all the people we interviewed for their valuable time and enriching discussion.

www.ingramcontent.com/pod-product-compliance
Lightning Source LLC
Chambersburg PA
CBHW050556280326
41933CB00011B/1862